Other Rooms

Neil Curry

Other Rooms
New and Selected Poems

ENITHARMON PRESS

First published in 2007
by Enitharmon Press
26B Caversham Road
London NW5 2DU

www.enitharmon.co.uk

Distributed in the UK by
Central Books
99 Wallis Road
London E9 5LN

Distributed in the USA and Canada
by Dufour Editions Inc.
PO Box 7, Chester Springs
PA 19425, USA

ISBN: 978-1-904634-44-7

Enitharmon Press gratefully acknowledges the financial support of
Arts Council England, London.

British Library Cataloguing-in-Publication Data.
A catalogue record for this book is available
from the British Library.

Designed in Albertina by Libanus Press
and printed in England by
Antony Rowe Ltd

for
Natasha and Victoria

ACKNOWLEDGEMENTS

Some of the *New Poems* first appeared in the following publications: *Illuminations, The Liberal, PN Review, Poetry London, Poetry Review, The Reader, The Red Letter, Scintilla, The Third Way.*

My thanks also go to The Blue Mountain Center; The Liguria Study Center, Bogliasco; The Virginia Center for the Creative Arts; and Yaddo.

CONTENTS

THE WELL

Though he leant right out over the rim,
The water was too far down for him to see.

'Time, you realise,' someone remarked
Inside his head, 'is only the rate

At which the past decays.' And so,
He let slip slowly through his fingers

The one or two choice memories he chanced
To have about him, then stood listening

Attentively for their depleted echo.

AN INVITATION

'Should you ever change your mind and decide
to visit me,' she had written, 'by far
the wisest way would be to come by water.
Of course, when the hibiscus is in flower,
the paths that lead up from the lower foothills
would be delightful, but after that one's faced
full-on by the whole San Telmo range,
which simply has to be climbed. There is no
way round it. Added to which, the rock face,

being shale, can, so I'm told, be quite
unstable when it rains. And it does rain too.
No, I'd rather far you came by water.
The packet-boat will bring you to the first
of the shallows, where the village people,
forewarned, will have a raft already built
for you. Few, it would seem, having ever
travelled as far up as the rapids. Thank them,
but somehow buy or borrow a canoe.

I should so envy you. Late evenings
spent along the river, when quiet mouths
come down to drink, are, as you'll find, among
the gentlest life can offer. But you must
travel light. No books. No. And please, do not
bother your brains by trying to think what
gifts to bring me. I want for nothing
here, save for the sound of your voice
talking to me – or better still – singing.'

AT LE CAFÉ DE LA GARE

The table they'd been shown to was so small
They could have easily reached out to slap
Each other across the face, had they had

A mind to. At least they were in the shade
Now, out of the glare of alternatives.
Weighed down by leisure, they sat and waited.

Rehearsed, 'S'il vous plaît, un mille feuille
And deux tasses de thé.' The silence bulged
But failed to burst. It was as if all this

Had taken place a year or more ago
And only through some glitch of memory
Was of concern to them. And there were still

The qualms of evening to be got through yet.

from a funeral and draws the curtains
against the frivolity of the sun.
July, it has to be said, is not one
of the more considerate times of year
to die, causing one's friends to dress in black
and stand around outside all afternoon.

Nevertheless, it had all gone off
quite swimmingly, most notably the sermon,
when the Reverend Mr Riley told them
they would meet up with Cicely again
one day, 'in another place'. That was nice.
She did though harbour some misgivings
about the need for Mr Riley
to be there – what with his halitosis.

Life was that much daintier without men.
Mind you, George was very considerate these days.
No, for Emma, heaven would be herself,
Augusta (now that she knew her place), Jane
and Harriet, on a Tuesday afternoon,
shortly before four o'clock, when Betty
brought the tea things in. Betty, yes and cook too,
would be forever indispensable of course,

but seemed contented with their lot
so would no doubt prove equally
amenable in Paradise. Paradise:
a plate of sandwiches, a pot of tea,
Darjeeling preferably, milk and sugar.
Well, perhaps not sugar in view of where
it came from. One would hardly want… nor that

Mr Cadwallader, such a pretentious
name for such a dumpy little man;
but then milk was not essential either.
One could learn to like lemon, given time.

The wrongly placed (as it had seemed to him)
Apostrophe got up upon its several
Tiny feet, strode purposefully across

The margin and began a traverse
Of the ridges of his index fingernail.
In the meantime, Miles had passed his arm

Around his little sister and was reading
To her as they walked together, up and down,
In the garden. No doubt an English

Garden with flowerbeds – nothing to match
The Villa Rincon and its high, cool terraces,
The grey-green leaves of the olive trees

Set off by the wrinkling blue of the sea.
Page fifty-six was where his marker was.
The children had evidently gone inside.

But not the pair of ladies, who were deep
In agitated conversation. Fifty-eight.
The cicadas had stopped, leaving behind

One of those silent moments when the world
Seems to have gathered itself together
And be crouching. The younger of the ladies

Was threatening to leave. A pine cone dropped,
And he had the uneasy feeling there was
Someone else looking out from underneath

His eyelids and leaning their elbows
(Could it be Quint?) on the sills of his skull.
And in that instant nothing seemed to him

More natural than that these things, as he
Had read somewhere, should be those other things
Which clearly they were absolutely not.

MRS ARNOLD HUTCHINSON CROSSES THE ARCTIC CIRCLE

Bare-breasted they were too for the most part
Those old figureheads, and she could sympathise
With them as she stood there up at the front

Outfacing the wind, the wet and the cold,
Watching the great white bow waves splintering
Into facets of cut jade as they broke

And slid by on either side. The icebergs
She would always remember, yes and those
Streaks of an almost delphinium blue

Some showed along the waterline; so huge
And yet so much submerged; like memories.
She'd forgotten just how unendurable

Memories could be when we can no longer
Pick and choose among them to suit ourselves.
The indifferent sea closed behind them

And soothed away all traces of their wake,
But she sensed that she had only to wait,
Wait for that oily, lacquered look the waves

Took on late of an afternoon and then
Something, she knew, *'The birds mark the place there!*
Mark the birds!' would breach and come boiling up

Among them, the waters spilling from its back,
Something she would gladly send her harpoon
Singing into, something for Queequeg

To get a rope around, winch on board
And haul onto the after-deck, where she herself
Could set about it with her flensing knives.

BENEATH THE WAVE OFF KANAGAWA

More than a little saddened

Saddened? I was outraged

by his grandson having gambled away

So prodigal and so very vulgar

those few handfuls of coins

and it was more than that.

which in a long, hard life
he had managed to gather together,
Katsushika Hokusai,

Close. Yes, not bad at all.

fearful now of penury,
tipped an old brush with a new

They said it was Prussian.

pigment and sent the first
flourish of 'The Great Wave'

off Kanagawa.
Will you get it right, please.

looping in one joyous arc
across the page. Mount Fuji
reduced to just another whitetop
underneath it, but far, far away.

You noticed that.

but then the spindrift tumbling from it
took on the look of claws

I suppose so

threatening

though I wouldn't go that far.

to engulf the little boats,
thin as laths, that were threading
their way among its troughs,
and overwhelming the huddled oarsmen,
those tiny, white-faced dolls

Heroes they were, man, heroes.

sending them to their doom.

Going with the flow.

What Hokusai has given us
is the steadiness of bafflement,
the incandescent poise, as it were,
of the hummingbird.

Yes, now that is very true.
I did.

Anyway, we were here first, and well settled in long before they showed up. There were leopards and lions loping through the long grass, and the centipedes and the woodlice had reached an agreement on whatever space might be domesticated under the damper stones. Then they arrived. Talking all the time and strutting about. I could see the chimps eyeing them up and shaking their heads, as if to say, 'They could catch their deaths, they could those two, going about like that.'

*

After a while they did deign to notice some of us. First it was the cats. She was always playing with the cats. The little ones, I mean. They were both a bit cagey about the bigger ones. Then it seemed he was incapable of going anywhere without a dog. Yet there were some of us they could not tolerate: spiders for one, which was hardly rational considering the ambiguous relationship they enjoyed with snakes.

*

The odd thing though was that it was quite a while before we realized they'd gone, and truth to tell there were more than a few of us who weren't too bothered, who'd always bridled a bit at the condescending way they had handed out names. It was all so arbitrary. Well, imagine being dubbed *unicorn* while others were called dolphin, gazelle and kittiwake. Before the week was out though, the vast majority had followed after them like sheep, and apart from myself, my friend the hippogriff, a family of basilisks, some firedrakes and a manticore, the place was soon almost deserted. Not that it stayed that way of course. The giant moa lost no time whatsoever in coming home, nor the aurochs. Then there was the great auk, and the Antarctic wolf, and I have it on good authority that the white rhinoceros will shortly be back among us. Them too I shouldn't wonder. Yes, up the hill they'll come, hand in hand with wandering steps and slow.

OTHER ROOMS

Afterwards, all he could remember clearly
Was the sound that the rain made, splattering
Against the paper wrappers of the flowers

Someone had been arranging around her grave.
He turned away from the window. When people
Are always there one tends to forget them.

And moved a cushion, but did not sit.
To be *gone*, a person needs to have been,
To be somebody something once happened to.

He thought perhaps to make some tea. When
There is not love enough to go around,
It ought to be the dead who go without.

Another room, another frontier. There would
Be others: stairs and doors. He could
Recall their bodies' fond acquaintanceship.

These were her gloves. Something akin,
He guessed, to immortality lay in his longing.
Elsewhere would be her shoes, and other things.

MONTICELLO

You have to look closely, but it's there
on the obverse of the nickel:
Jefferson's Monticello among the loose change
in your pocket. Such a cheapskate
tribute I always think to the man
who ditched the pound in favour of the dollar.

Waiting to greet us on the steps
of the portico, our guide proved to be
a master of alliteration.
'In 1809,' he told us, 'the President
quit the purgatory of politics
for this pastoral paradise.'
There was more too,
but I lost it among the studied
grandiloquence of his gestures,
his stage-managed mannerisms.

Waved inside, we were in what seemed
more of a museum than a home:
maps and minerals,
peace-pipes and wampum belts,
even the jaw-bone of a mastodon.

He had seen himself as a second Horace:
'I had rather be shut up
in a very modest cottage with my books...'
but it had taken all of eighty-six
packing cases to ship his furniture
back home from Paris – those Louis XVI
fauteuils en cabriolet.

Acquisitive as a squirrel he was, yet I
who have never knowingly passed by

a secondhand bookshop, have to admire
a man whose personal library
ran close to seven thousand volumes,
and this before Barnes and Noble
or even Amazon.

Books and clocks.
'It is wonderful how much may be done
if one is always doing.'
And he was. He could step
straight from his bed into the clutter
of his office and sit at his beloved
Hawkes and Peale Polygraph, a machine
which allowed him to write a letter with one hand
while an invisible amanuensis
made a copy of it with another.

In his dining room, dumb waiters
and revolving shelves ensured
that other hands stayed equally invisible.
The simple life is easy to extol
when you are rich enough, but it's hard
to say if 'the pursuit of happiness'
is the same as being happy.

There was no mention made of the shacks
that once lined Mulberry Row
or of the children living out there
that Sally Hemmings bore him.

He was after all a politician,
a man, therefore, who could be counted upon
to keep a secret, even from himself.

They were leaving
as heathen as they'd come.

He had half hoped
one might return his part-wave, part-blessing.
It was still early of course,
and cowled in his long black robe
he could, he supposed, have been taken
for another shadow and no thing of substance.

He would miss them – there was no doubt of that –
these masons, carpenters and quarrymen;
their womenfolk too – wives, they said,
whores, they were; he knew that much.

Not that it had ever been easy.
Those raucous songs they'd bawled out
in counterpoint against the Eucharist;
and that gargoyle – it had looked far too much
like poor old brother Anselm to be funny.

Untouched they might have been
by what they'd done, but just look
at what it was they'd done.

And there was something about their noisy
camaraderie he had it in himself to envy,
the fearlessness, their nonchalant
agility, even at the dizziest of heights.

The fluidity of things had always been
what most entranced him,
how, as seasons came and went, each ring
of green wood toughened into heartwood.

Stone by stone,
amid a reek of beer
and onions that had outdone
whatever incense he might burn,
the abbey slowly had assumed its shape,
until, like that moment in an hour of prayer
when world and self cohere, the time had come
when every stitch of scaffolding was
taken down and there it stood,
'prepared as a bride adorned
for her husband'
{*Revelation*, Chapter 21, Verse 2}.

There was no room for excuses any more.
Consummatum est, he had half caught himself
thinking, and flinched. Light began to play
across the windows of the new scriptorium.

Yes, it was high time he faced up to the word.

THE WEATHER HOUSE

I've just seen my neighbour go indoors
carrying a basket of fruit
and a bunch of flowers.
It has started to rain.
I wonder if her husband will come out
in his wellies and raincoat
and stand on the steps
until it stops
and he can go inside again.

1812 – OVERTURE AND CLOSURE

I

Tchaikovsky himself soon fell out of love
With it: the predictable booms of the big guns,
And those altogether-too-ecstatic bells.

Moscow burning, and the slow French trudge back
Through a frozen land was more the truth of it.
At 30 below they fought over fires.

Ate their own horses. Some, looking up, glimpsed
A slight smudge in the night sky – *The Great Comet* –
Took it for an ill omen, and died standing.

II

May 25th. Jarrow. Nigh on noon. Nothing
But broken cloud over Felling Pit. No comet.
It is one thousand and seventy-seven years

To the day since Bede died here, *borne aloft*
By angels. Below ground it's change-over time.
The earth mutters; first one seam then another

Explodes, sending debris, dust and coal higher and
Higher, while ninety-two men and boys, having no
Room to stand, are burned to death, mostly crouching.

A WORD WITH BEDE

'Hac sunt in fossa Baedae venerabilis ossa'
   (words over Bede's tomb in Durham Cathedral)

I've always liked that story of the monk
Carving your tombstone, and being at a loss
For words, well for an adjective at least,

To put in front of *bones* – so he left a gap,
And overnight an angel came and filled it in
With *venerabilis* – a name (it does now

Seem to be your name) that's really stuck.
There's something sort of mildewed though
About Venerable; it makes me think

Of *verdigris*, as if your Benedictine robe
Weren't always quite as fresh as it might have been,
And makes you seem perpetually old,

Which of course you weren't. Another story
Has it you were the little lad 'nourished and taught'
By Ceolfrith, you and he the only survivors

When that Third Rider – plague – trampled down Jarrow.
Frightening for a child it must have been: those buboes
Big as apples, the retching and the deadly

Ring o' roses before the skin turned black.
Thanks be your own death was more gentle.
As you said: having lived without shame

You could die without fear. But managing
To hold on until you'd finished translating John,
That was a nice touch – those closing words of his:

'I suppose that even the world itself
Could not contain the books that should be written.'
How many you yourself had written

I suppose we will never know. Alone
In your cell with your lampblack ink, and pens,
Recounting the exploits of the saints –

Their voyages, their miracles and derring-do –
There were times when you doubted whether what you'd done
Had been enough, you who'd never ventured

Further than Lindisfarne, and that only once,
While so many of your friends had made their way
To Rome and back. But you were the maker. Without

You, we would never have known of the otters
That came running to dry St Cuthbert's feet
With their fur when he'd been praying in the sea;

Or of Edwin's thane likening our lives
To the flight of a sparrow – coming from
A howling winter's storm into the light

And warmth of the mead hall, where great lords
Sat feasting, then straightway out into the storm again;
Or of the poet Caedmon who fled

From the song only to be found by the Singer.
Only books? Bede, hinny, you showed us miracles
Can flare out from so little as the turning of a page.

AMONG THE RUINS

Do mind how you go up this path. Myself,
I quite like the way these clumps of wizened
Hawthorn grow like bonsai from out the clefts
In the limestone, but it would be only
Too easy to miss your footing. There aren't
That many of us come up here these days.

Well, no, you're right, there aren't many of us
Still remember them – leastways not firsthand.
It strikes me as odd now, considering
What little notice they took of us, but we
Felt secure just knowing they were up there,
Yet if we chanced somehow to rile them,

Even unbeknown, oh by God they came down
Hard on us then I can tell you. We'd do
What we could to appease them, offering
Up things I suppose they had no need of,
But it made no difference. They never
Even deigned to tell us they were going.

No, we none of us heard or saw a thing.
One morning there was just this queasy silence.
We couldn't fathom what was happening.
We felt lost. Were we free? If so, freedom's
A far cry from what it's cracked up to be.
We were desolate. Of course our youngsters

Grew up knowing nothing different, but
Some my age have never settled. It's like
An amputated limb they feel after.
Well, here we are then. This is what you came
To see. I wouldn't go too far inside
If I were you though; that masonry looks

None too safe. At night sometimes we hear it
Falling. It's frost gets into it, I'm told.
What folks to come will make of it I can't
Imagine. The halls of giants possibly.
So, shall I just leave you to wander round?

SHUTTING DOWN

When they moved his chair nearer the window
They told him he had to take things easy.
Easy? What in blazes was there out there for him
To see, let alone excite him? Some oaks
Down by the lake, and the big house over
On the other side. Since early June though

There'd been no end of goings-on: music,
And that non-stop laughter of an evening
When they brought their drinks out on the lawn.
Feckless – that was the word which sprang to mind.
Yet, even so, he had enjoyed the way
The flimsy dresses of that dark-haired girl

Would twirl and flare out as she danced or ran.
All summer long the same; till Friday last
When they had packed themselves, bag and baggage,
Into their several motor cars, tooted,
And were gone. Come Saturday, he saw
Two men in workday clothes tidying up,

And making fast the shutters. Indoors,
He could assume, they'd turned the water off
And drained the central heating. Cold weather
Must be on its way. Soon enough he'd hear
The wild geese flying overhead. Not that
Nothing of interest had been happening

Nearer home. Day by day the trees had been
Turning sunlight into chlorophyll and hauling
Water up some sixty feet or more with the
Minimum of fuss, producing acorns
By the barrowful. Lately though they seemed
To have severed all connection with their leaves.

Away they went, yellow, tan and russet,
Flickering over the waters of the lake.
He watched them go. Were little children,
He wondered, still taught that catching one
Before it touched the ground was a sure sign of
Long life? No, wait; it might have meant good luck.

IN A CALENDAR OF SAINTS

I

Wondering which of all the saints
Had been assigned to share the hours with me
On this the first day of February
(The snow beginning to thaw outside
As though touched by these jets of flame-blue
Hyacinth burning in the window)
I found not one name but two: Ignatius
Of Antioch, and Saint Brigid.

Arrested, and shipped in fetters
Back to Trajan's Rome, Ignatius,
Intent upon martyrdom, begged
That no-one intercede for him. 'I am
God's own grain,' he wrote, pausing
Among his strictures on the Trinity
And Eucharist, 'and will prove good bread
Though ground in the jaws of the arena's beasts.'

But in Kildare, there was no lion's tooth,
Just the dandelion: Brigid's flower.
Patron of things new-born, who turned water
Into milk, not wine, hers is the other
Face of the world. And on Candlemas Eve
She comes to us with her lambs, quickening
The year: abbess and triple-goddess;
Bride the Beautiful: the Celtic Muse.

II

With Concordius their first foot, the saints
Go marching through the pages of the year:
Hermits and founders of great orders,
Contemplatives, and martyrs to the faith:
Men like Aquinas, most learned of the saints
And most saintly of the learned;
Or that other Thomas, whose turbulent brain
Richard le Breton splattered
Over the altar-cloth at Canterbury.

Some, looking for nothing from this world,
Were, like Cuthbert, content that it should shrink
To a rock off Lindisfarne, where grey seals
Bobbed up and blinked their nostrils in surprise;
While in Assisi, Francis could not embrace
Or bless enough of it, were it his Lady
Poverty or the leper's hand. Almost blind,
In the convent garden of San Damian
He sang his *Canticle of Brother Sun*:

A chorus of witness in which we hear
Pointers to what may, impossibly,
Prove possible: as when in August 1941,
On the Eve of the Feast of the Assumption,
Maximilian Kolbe, Polish priest,
In the starved dark of Cell Block 13
Took upon himself another man's death;
The carbolic acid sluiced through his veins
Winning one more victory for Golgotha.

POPPY HEADS

There is, it seems, no poppy seed so old
That given a drop of water and some warmth
It will not flower again, breaking the dream
Of its opiate sleep to send new fancies
Shimmering along the blood. After twenty
Centuries, when smart industrialists
Moved back into the silver mines at Laurium
To pocket up the banks of spoil heaps,
There was a moment's hesitation

In the dust, then wild and exotic
Poppy buds came powering up – strange sons
And daughters of blooms that Pliny must have known,
And would have seen stamped out in tesserae
Upon the Aventine, and on the portly
Bellies of black amphorae: Ceres' sign;
Shocks of sheer scarlet in a yellow heat
That twined through stooks and burned against the blue:
Manna for the mind beside the body's bread.

But what was manna? The word was no more
Than a mute echo that tried to give
A miracle a name. All they could tell
Was that it came after the quails had flown in
With the falling of the dusk and settled
Over the Wilderness of Sin: a gift
From an otherwise indifferent night
In answer to their needs, their dream; and now
An image of the fulfilment of a dream.

For dreams are not caught in the dissonant
Thickets of language, nor strung on time's links;
They come to us with all the inseminate
Anarchy of the image, and every mote
Of the past concurrent, so wherever
A poppy head has nodded in the world
Some seed may lie waiting and from the pit of night
Will delight, bewilder or admonish us
With the ambiguous innocence which is its power.

GARDENS

We smiled together
over the precepts in that old herbal,
vowing, as we valued our eyesight,
    never to gather
   the fruit of the peony
    save at dead of night
and thus 'all unseene of the woodpecker',

    noted too that powdered
periwinkle and earthworm, if taken
at mealtimes, does rekindle a wife's
    love for her husband;
   strange that they would tolerate
    such wild beliefs
in days when heretics, not weeds, got burned.

    But what gardeners they were;
what arbours of trellis work; embroidered
intricacies of bright nose-gay knots;
    thrift and lavender-
   scented walks of evergreen;
    what salves and syrops
of simple herbs for health and provender;

    what workers for Eden.
Though few of us today would freely voice
our dreams of unicorns and rosebuds,
    their secret garden
   has alleyways that may yet
    outpace all our thoughts.
What our lives lack is what our hands fashion.

The Mogul emperor
Babur blazed and butchered his way across
the steppes of Asia, then called a halt
while his warriors
erected walls around one
cool sequestered spot
where lilacs shaded white shawls of water.

THE MAIDENHAIR TREE

It was a tree that neither
    of us had ever seen before,
its trunk lined and grey, its leaves
like little pairs of green webbed feet
    and strangely fleshy;

but what really stopped us as we stepped
    from stained-glass cloistered gloom
into impartial sunlight?
Remembering Thoreau saying
    how monstrous he thought

it was that people cared so little
    about trees, yet so much
for Corinthian columns?
Or the affront of namelessness,
    the one challenge

capable of overwhelming knowledge,
    in that its secret lies
not in saying but being;
and not the tawdry masquerades
    of reverie, the

fictions and fripperies of longing,
    but plainly and truly
what for the beholder *is*:
the embodiment of the one
    moment; for language

however deftly it may be used
   in the flora, will not
explain the susurrations
of dry leaves, and illustration,
   though perfect of line,

shows nothing of the rings' slow stretching
   and splitting, the great thirst
sucking moisture from the black
earth to breathe it out through the green
   veins of its foliage:

but such realities always must
   admit experience,
not just the thing perceived but
the experience likewise of
   the perceiving mind,

so that tree now cannot simply be
   without the cathedral
close we first found it in, and
our shared memories, both of which
   lie beyond telling.

CAVE PAINTINGS

How did the old hands come by this colour
(that glint of copper late autumn sunshine
   gives to dying bracken)
for the flanks of these portly little
   low-slung Chinese horses here?

Ground haematite, ochre or whatever?
But look how that slight bulge in the rock face
   has so fleshed a rib-cage
one half-hears the clatter of their black
   (as stamen of tulips) hooves

go galloping off down the passageways.
Turning to watch them though, you're faced with the
   blunt head of a great bull
aurochs, glaring and snorting out of
   the swirling smoke of his mane.

But beyond all this – the charcoal mammoth
and the herds of ibex – comes the painted
   palm-print. A signature?
The simple affirmation of self?
   A greeting or a ritual?

What does seem clear is that, of the claws, teeth,
antlers, horns, talons and tusks of the dark,
   he had no fear at all ...
or so this would have us believe. Our
   simpler wish: not not to be?

TO THE GLASS-BLOWERS

The problem is one of how to paint
An empty wineglass in full sunlight
On a windowsill so as to capture

Those complicities of glass and light
Which at times suggest the glass may be
A consummation of the spirit

Of the light, even while it flings
It off in prism; to capture
Not only the essence and the past

But also the potential; not simply
What things are, but the power of what
They might just possibly become:

The quest which, with their retorts and stills,
Their crucibles and limbecks, alchemists
From Paracelsus down to Jonson's Subtle

All set themselves, pitting opposite against
Elemental opposite in that secret war,
And so busily they never noticed

How in Venice, craftsmen in overalls
Were putting earth – through sand and potash –
To a trial by fire, and their gaffer,

As they called him, once that red
Gob of the metal was twirling through his fingers,
Breathed into it of his own human spirit.

SHIPS IN BOTTLES

You've seen paper when it's burnt
And turned to ash, yet keeps its shape,

How fine it is? Well, the sails
Were like that, and the rigging

Something spiders might have spun:
Royals from fore to mizzen,

Delicacy and precision overall;
But a touch of fury too

Where the painted figure-heads
Fought through the foam.

And their maker?

No salty tar sitting on the quay
With the tops of his sea-boots rolled.

No, he kept bees, grew begonias,
Lived alone, and never complained.

Why then these vessels – bottled wanderers
Bobbing on a sideboard sea?

Uncorked, might a bright sprite pop out
To meet all wishes, or would it

Be some gaunt Ahab – black
From the scorch of hell –

Cursing the storms that howled inside?

LINDISFARNE

All afternoon a cold east wind
Had parched the sand to a smooth, scraped vellum
That the cursive run of the tide
Would scrawl across, stipple and etch.
Later, when it had all but
Covered Cuddy's Rock, the dark cormorants
Hung out their wings to dry.

From his scriptorium window
Eadfrith had sketched their great beaks and pebbled
Luxury of that beach. Now though
There was Jerome's *Prolegomena*
To be penned. 'Novum opus
Facere me cogis ex verteri...'
New work out of the old.

For such tasks, tired dexterities
Are never enough; echoes of echoes.
What's called for is that other gift
Which subverts logic with all the
Nonchalance of nuance: a man
Conscious of the silence flooding his mind
And giving voice to it.

Whirlpools of ribboned interlace
He drew, maelstroms of colour: indigo,
Verdigris, orpiment and woad;
Labyrinths and carpets of praise,
Of spirals, eyed-pelta and plait.
Craftsman, peacock and saint, Eadfrith's
Quills fluttered with the Word.

GALAPAGOS

With FitzRoy's twenty-two chronometers
Ticking on their shelves, Darwin, sick again,
Killed time re-reading Lyell's *Geology*,
Or *Paradise Lost* – his favourite poem.

On deck the crew were plump and happy now.
Roast armadillo and ostrich dumplings
Had brought them round Cape Horn, and the *Beagle*,
Under full sail, was tacking for the Line.

But charting that long, sheep's jaw-bone of a coast
Could not assuage the zealot in FitzRoy.
To substantiate the Flood, evidence
For Genesis: that was what he wanted.

When they landed, Antediluvian
Was at every turn, but nowhere Eden:
Not in such heat; not with such contortions
Of cinder and lava; and not with such

Black imps of Hell as the iguanas
Crawling and slithering about these blighted
Encantadas, these Enchanted Islands,
Where the chief sound of life was a hiss,

From the snakes, and from the giant tortoises,
The indomitable *galapagos* themselves,
As they lurched and lumbered their way inland
Following their ancient paths to water.

Yet in all this new weird, it was the beaks
Of brown finches that dismasted FitzRoy,
And sent him on his solitary way
To slash a red equator round his throat.

ST KILDA

I

The map the domine had tacked up
On the schoolroom wall didn't even show
St Kilda, but then only a foreigner
Would have needed one to find his way past Mull
And Skye, out through the Sound of Harris, then on
For fifty empty miles over the
Oily pitch and swell of the grey
North Atlantic.
                         Any St Kildans,
Out of sight of land, with bad weather closing,
Knew they'd only to watch the flight-paths
Of the birds: guillemot and gannet would wreck them
On the stacs round Boreray, while puffins
Scuttering back wave-high to Dun
Would prove a safe guide home to Hirta
And the Village Bay.

II

Birds. Or angels even
They must have seemed, the women
Plucking, in a cloud of feathers,
At the haul of fulmar their menfolk

Had themselves plucked off the cliffs
Of Conachair; cragsmen spidering
Thirty fathoms down, along ledges
Of guano, dependent on sheer faith

In their neighbours and on a horsehair rope.
Claim life those cliffs could, but always would
Sustain it while there were sea-birds
In such thousands to stew or dry;

Even a gannet's neck, turned inside out,
Made a snug boot, and oil from the fulmar
Not only fuelled their lamps, but was a panacea
For no matter what ills or ailments of the island.

III

Ultima Thule it was
Until the Victorians discovered it,
Sending in their missionaries
To pound out the parable

Of the Prodigal Son
To people who hadn't
Anywhere to stray to
And had never seen a pig.

Then steamers came, and summer visitors
With gimcrack charities and new disease,
Tipping the cragsmen with a penny each
To see them capering about on Conachair;

Pennies the winter ferryman
Would finger from the eyelids of their dead.

IV

By lantern-light
They loaded a few more
Sticks of furniture
And the last of the sheep,
And then they drowned their dogs.

In the morning,
According to custom,
In every empty house
There was a Bible left
Open at Exodus.

THE PLAIN PEOPLE

I

About a mile off Highway 7
down the road to Conestoga,
the land becomes good:
good, fertile land,
where the earth
would almost stain your fingers;
black earth it is, and with a sheen
to match that on the thick
coats of the horses that come now
walking warily from winter barns
out onto the fresh fields;
for these are Mennonite fields,
and at the ends of lanes
their mail boxes – one half expects
Black Letter – preach out the names:
Amos Eby, Menno Martin,
Noah Hoyt and all the host
of Brubacher that came
from Pennsylvania in the wagons
a hundred years ago
to buy a mortgaged wilderness,
and stay 'unspotted from the world'.

II

For the Mennonites
the world was once the Netherlands,
till God's own vigilantes
beat, broke, and beheaded them;
was Germany, till they were burned
for accursed Anabaptists,

their womenfolk buried alive –
witness Fräulein von Hove's friends
stamping on the ground above her head
to help her die. But the New World
ends the obligation for martyrdom.

III

Pacifists, where peace now
has become anachronistic,
they struggle to preserve
some placid image of their past:
in broad-brimmed hats
and plain black clothes
they drive their buggies
through the lines of Pontiacs;
in their church a literal Bible
and a literal washing of feet.

IV

Drab, yet conspicuous
as a circus,
they tend their stalls
in Kitchener market,
stamping their feet
against the early morning cold –
the dollar is difficult to avoid –
offering up fruit and cookies,
embroidered pinafores, and jars
of Mother Martin's Apple Butter
'made from a recipe
five generations old'.

V

Five generations of shadows,
shadows of martyrs and travellers,
shadows of farmers
and hewers of trees,
they have inherited the names,
and inherited the clothes,
but with them have put on
a terrible purposeless peace,
an all-embracing denial.
In-bred to the point of idiocy
and seeming to glory in it,
they hold their high-stepping horses
on a mean rein.

THE DOLL'S HOUSE

Open the doors
and let your little fat pinkies
prowl through these rooms.

There is no cellar
with dark stairs
to frighten the children.

It is a house
with no roots at all.
Come into the hall

and tap the barometer
that hangs on the wall.
It will neither rise nor fall.

In the kitchen
you will touch
the little red paper fire

that glows in the range,
then put your finger
to your mouth

and make a show
of being burned.
They all do.

And you may,
if you will,
mumble my wooden food.

Upstairs, in the bedroom,
you will not fail
to lift up the pretty valance

and find
to your feigned
and loud delight

that there is indeed
a guzunder there.
For this is an old house

and as its ways
are not your ways,
improprieties

are of no account.
But when you find me
and try to lift me,

as I know you will,
you will find
that someone –

oh, it was years ago –
thought fit to stitch me
into my chair.

KINGFISHER

If Christ our king could
In the ammoniac stench of the stable
Suffer at His Nativity to be
Neighbour to slow-breathing beasts,

Then small wonder that the king-
fisher's spark should be struck
In a damp underworld of willow root and worm
Where vole and water-rat splash.

For once the shells split and sapphire
And fire-opal fledge in their filth
And six or seven small spurts of flame
Are tumbled out into the dazzle,

Then earth, air, fire and water meet
In a perfection of balance, trafficking,
Like prayer, between this world and that.
And isn't it then that their mother's

Fabled and other self is said to brood
On a nest of bones, calming the waters,
And granting us glimpses of Eden
In those Mary-blue halcyon days?

MUTE SWANS

Why did Ben Jonson
               like a great battle fleet
Call Shakespeare
               line astern they come
A swan?
               down the river,
And of Avon too
               breaking the water
When he spent the whole of his working life
               with their silence,
By the Thames?
               and such power
He must have seen him
               in a bird,
At Stratford, I suppose,
               the great paddles of their feet
When he'd downed his quill
               working away under the surface,
And wondered at such silence
               these mute swans

FOUR TIMES FOUR

I
The coincidence of spring
and dawn: but was that
a child watching the fires
to the east,

II
or a young girl
in the full noon of summer,
turning her face
to feel the southern breeze?

III
With the children asleep now,
her ears caught the sound
of water running westward
one autumn evening.

IV
She felt her age
crossing the cold yard in the dark;
thought she could smell snow
on the hills to the north.

THE CREATION OF CAEDMON

The open fires flung giant shadows
Onto the walls behind them: great black monks
Louring over the kindly, venerable men
Who sang and passed the harp
One man to the next down the long table.

The shadows were only shadows, but Caedmon,
Shivering under their menace, knew
That the strings were closing in to torture him
And he scrambled out into the safety of starlight
To stand a moment, leaning his back

Against the abbey door before stepping carefully
Over the icy cobbles to his bed in the stable,
Where the beasts that night were grumbling
Softly at their trough, and the song waiting
Inexorably for His new singer.

ANNE HATHAWAY COMPOSES
HER 18TH SONNET

I wonder what I ought to do today.
This autumn weather's still so temperate
You'd almost think that it was early Maie
And that we'd somehow muddled up the date.
I've polished all the silver till it shines;
Some bits were tarnish'd, all their sheen quite dimm'd.
I'd like some help, but Will always declines,
Says, 'Can't you see the hedge is still untrimm'd?'
I really think our love's begun to fade.
He nags me so. 'The milliner thou ow'st,'
He says, 'and did we need that new lampshade?
It's not on trees you know that money grow'st.'
 And then he's off to London with, 'I'll see
 You, chuck. Now don't you fret. I'll write to thee!'

GEORGE FOX CROSSES THE BAY

On the beach at Bardsea, the cocklewomen
Stood watching, waiting, dry-eyed for them to drown.
Around their horses' hooves a rip-tide was racing
And swirling away the brogs of gorse

That had marked safe-passage over the sands,
So now it was too late even for them to turn.
But that speck against the dark sky,
What was it? Was it a star rising?

Was it a sign? Later they would tell
How the great God Himself had parted
The waters; how that Quaker hat of his,
That stayed, God save us, undoffed

Even at Swarthmoor, had been a halo
Round his head; would bear witness
To the grit that lodged in the hard shells
Of their cockled hearts as he rode towering by.

JOHN WESLEY AMONG THE MINERS

The dirt, dear God, the squalor and the stench
Of those men; why, when one wept I will swear
That teardrop was the first water to touch
His face in weeks, and nothing but liquor
Down his gullet, I should think. And yet he did weep,
Shuddered and twitched too, like a hanged man on the rope,
But the rope that day was the Lord's and hauled
Not at his neck but his immortal soul.

Such was the spectacle; God's great drama:
Unlooked-for grace that grasped a sinner's life
And shook it as any man might shake a
Stopped clock upon the kitchen mantelshelf
To get it going; then how they chimed out when Charles
Set the rich wafer of his words upon their tongues,
And stole from the devil those enchanting tunes.
We fished in the ditches, but we brought back pearls.

LET CHRISTOPHER REJOICE

For although he is to die of drink and debt
    in the King's Bench,
He is dried out now and singing for David.

For whereas the watchmen in St James's Park would
    strike him down with their staffs,
Here at least they let him pray without ceasing.

For although 'Silly fellow! Silly fellow!' they
    call him,
He has a garden with pinks to tend, and in his room
    paper and pens enough for *Jubilate Agno*
    to grow daily.

For although the rat has bit poor Jeoffry's
    throat,
The considerations of this cat will become
    immortal.

For although Nancy and her daughters deserted
    poor Kit,
All the beasts, birds, fish, flowers and gems of
    the world will worship and rejoice with him
    in his own Magnificat.

For whereas God once bent back His bow to smite
    down His enemies,
Christopher has undertaken to re-write His Psalms
    and is now wearing, like a scarf around him,
    the exultant rainbow of His Love.

Emmonsales Heath was the last rim of the world.
A child could see that. Once there he would kneel
And peer down over the dreadful edge of it
And learn its secrets. Just one good day's walk
Was all it needed. But night, closing in,
Found his feet tired and turning for home.

Next it was the Enclosures Man who baulked him,
Fencing the land with lines of quickthorn
And leaving him only the plod of words
To get there – words which Taylor would root up
And level out, planting crops of commas
That tore like thistles through his thoughts.

So hedged about, where else was there to go?
Safer indoors perhaps with Dr Prichard...
He never could have guessed they meant to chop
Off his head and steal away his alphabet,
All those pretty vowels and consonants,
Tweezering them out, one by one, through his ears.

'Botany ... is a pursuit that amuses the fancy and exercises the memory, without improving the mind or advancing any real knowledge.'

Gilbert White

No, not more snow – just the petals from a windblown Blackthorn settling in the wet ruts of the lane.

LICHEN

At all frontiers;
over the tundra;
above the tree-line;

their blue-green frost
holds hard,
subdues bare stone,
battens on sour soil.

These are the pioneers,
mapping new ground,
flourishing their shields,
their grey rosettes.

Colonisers,
preparing the way
for what is merely huge,
they move on.

TOADSTOOLS

Who
in the night
severed
all these babies'

hands
and hid them
palms uppermost
under the

walnut tree?
This morning
there are tiny
fingers

and pudgy little
nail-less thumbs
around all its
damp roots.

PIMPERNEL

Allowing into the pharmacopoeia
of the fields
only what was held
to be useful,

savants said
these scarlet sparks
among the dust and chaff
would purge a melancholy;

and picked
with all the omens so
would grant you second-sight.
But what more witch-

or leech-craft could one wish
than eyes which blink out
days that break
a little damp and drear?

LILY OF THE VALLEY

Ego sum flos campi
et lilium convallium,
said Solomon
of this ladder-to-heaven lily.

Lovers in Paris wear it
as a corsage of constancy;
and drunken in the quantitie
of a sponeful

its water restoreth speech
and does strengthen memorie;
which only makes it the more
astounding that ten minutes

after four drops were jabbed
into the veins of some poor pooch
the dumb beast lay doggo –
aye, and in Paris too.

DANDELION

This is time's
(one o'clock, two o'clock)
golden head
wet the bed

flower;
forever turning its
(four o'clock, five o'clock)
face

to follow the sun.
But it's time that sets the
(seven o'clock, eight o'clock)
grey hairs growing

and will scythe off its
(eleven o'clock, twelve o'clock)
limp and wrinkled
ugly bald skull.

IVY

Gargoyle or saint
or blank grey wall
it's all
stone for the tendril.

Trees it chokes;
stifles
the sap's fluency.
Yet Pliny claims

a wreath of it
worn Bacchus-like
will counterpoise
the sway of wine.

Mournful
and magic plant
Horace and Virgil
took it for their crown.

FUNGUS

Spores
blowing into the dead
face of a felled birch
as it dries and splits

blossom as
orange freckles
and fine green hair;
or garish

fly agaric
blazing out of the mulch
where woodlice huddle
among crumpled ears

and shaggy parasols;
rampant in illusion,
the earth sucks
at its own insane root.

HAWTHORN

Bridewhite though it may be,
there is something
of the sweet stench
of lechery

about the hawthorn.
Mothers won't give it house-room:
unlucky – so they say.
And preachers warned

that the foulest putrefaction
of the plague pits
dwelt in its blossom –
that its smell was death.

But the brides of Beltane
still plucked it in armfuls,
wreathed it round their maypoles
and danced until they sweat.

'I am the solitude that asks and promises nothing;
that is how I shall set you free.'

PART I

1

And he thought of Sadak, poor Herculean mite
grappling wearily with that one last overhang;
     bewildered in a mountainscape
of Martinian confectionery
     and cataracts of caramel.

2

Why Sadak though, when surely these soft sandy slopes
would lead to no such waters of oblivion?
     This gave him pause, and his nostrils
narrowed, as they sensed some new shiver
     in the damp furrows of the wind.

3

Flexing his toes he heeled off down towards the beach,
where weed and shellfish crunched and squelched beneath his feet:
     the flung detritus of the sea,
whose creamy, thick and overlapping foam
     glushed and spluttered along the shore

4

with an empty, high-flown fury; swaggering up
only to cringe and snivel back again, leaving
     jots of unintelligible
marginalia scribbled there in brine;
     jots which even the stalky eyes

5

of crabs which plopped and popped open like brown bubbles
in the cold silt could take no readings from; patterns
   of marbled mottling and lace.
The dumb barbaric vagueness of it all
   was what appalled Alonso most.

6

On his sea of dreams sometimes, she had held out hopes
of handsome clipper fleets flying before the trades,
   harmonious concord of keels,
with their kelsons all humming like harp-strings
   and water curdled in their wake,

7

but crewed by practical men of affairs, these all
had harbours to get to, and did not feel disposed
   to lower gigs for castaways.
So when the western horizon came rolling
   in under them, he was left

8

to founder in his sleep. Yet still Alonso sensed
that though these dwellers on the deep might scorn his strand,
   it really was the only place
where one might dabble one's dry thumbs and feel
   the rhythms of each ocean's pulse.

PART II

9

Late November it had been when he'd first set out;
not the most auspicious time of year to begin
   such a journey, when all men else,
having greased their tools against the winter,
   seemed quite content to sit and think

10

of pocky mandarins and nuts; for November
is such a quiet and downtrodden kind of month;
    it lacks the clean finality
of cold, the brittle fern-frond-on-slate
    precision of its absolute.

11

But what weighed worse, his neighbours could almost have
been
the month itself, they'd such a damp and doubting air;
    their very silence lacked a voice,
was empty even of the unspoken
    resonances of those words

12

we have no need for when there's anguish near the bone.
Beset by nerves so taut a breath of wind could draw
    a chord from them, a man might well
luxuriate a while in such a peace,
    beatus ille, yet not for long;

13

the singing rocks are risky, but there's no quester
could survive their total and contemptuous mute;
    and the most myth that could be hoped
was that some kindly hand might hold an end
    while Orpheus tried to thread himself

14

through the labyrinthian eye of their nostalgia.
He knew himself climbing up out of the dark; slow
    and pensive, until his fingers
gripped the top rim of the ridge with first light.
    It was a morning neither blue

15

nor grey, the sky not a colour but a distance,
and he watched his long shadow go rippling down
    into the valley before him.
Descent was dire, but as the aggression
    of the ground grew less, knots of gorse

16

and writhen thorn gave way to quickbeam, birch and ash,
each branch as velvet as a young deer's horn, the hoarfrost
    had so textured them; and crisp grass
that squeaked underfoot as he neared his people
    numb in their circle of sallows.

PART III

17

As once in the valley of bones Ezekiel,
so now he, vocable life into their marrow
    breathed, and what toppled dolmen seemed
he moved: rue-leaved or starry saxifrage
    the word that bloomed among the stone.

18

Their gloomy world of course had long before been loud
and even odorous with a brutal kind of
    statement and reply, but the word
was like warm days to frozen fields, and waked
    the faint beginnings of a tune:

19

(purple of cello under emeralds of flute)
it came with a new bloom like the patina
    of brushed plum upon it, and so took
possession of the air, life leapt with it
    and feet lifted to the measure

20

dancing the gone of winter till even the reeds
that combed at the river's edge grew melodious,
    piping with the inspiration
of the breeze eclogues of lost Arcadies.
    There were no poems, only words,

21

yet all the words that were, were poems: the concert
of myth and tongue. For it was this: the wish for things
    as they could never quite be, this
and not a thin contingency of *is*,
    that on the blue plains of Shinar

22

energised the namer, in whose lost name this dark
ivy twists once more, climbing like the winding stair
    inside a tower, where you sit
reading by lamplight in the still quiet
    of calm. Instead though, read now of

23

an ancient rowan tree high up in the mountains,
with woodsmen working to fell it. See their iron
    axes vying with stroke after
juddering stroke to bring it down. See its leaves
    shiver, and how its topmost boughs

24

begin to tremble until, vanquished at last, it
keels over with a great groan and crashes, trailing
    its havoc down the mountain's side.
Well, it was the same with your tower too,
    and with Alonso's and with mine.

25

All rummaged in the rubble's billowing smokedust
blind, snatching up what fragments of old phrases
   they could find; the fall having torn
out tongues and cut the people at their root,
   each word lost was a whole world gone,

26

while some they saved had in themselves a savour
of mortality: the greenest inference of *was*
   tasted of ashes in their mouths
and one rhyme only could be found for breath.
   So Alonso ran beside them

27

scattering all the enticements of late summer
at their feet: eglantine and marigold and musk,
   but, as deep in every flower
that they gathered, they saw time's eyelid blink,
   what use to them was his fiction?

28

If he'd woven robes of opulent silk to fling
about their shoulders, all they'd have known was the worm
   and its itch. What did they want? Poems
that told them what they knew to be true, or
   was it the truth of poetry?

29

Which, as she always said, was to see that no one
forgot what they did not know they knew: the essence
   and not the aspect; the hard seed
and not the winnowable husk. And yet
   times there are when even a seed

30

feels inside itself the pressure of its own seeds
raging to wrinkle what as yet's not ripe. Then dumb
    fear of the flail comes, men moping
at a harvest home; for after the sound
    of the deep bass-viol is done

31

and the topers have lurched off home through the darkness,
there is only the darkness; midwinter silence,
    madness or suicide: coldest
and echoic limit of all language.
    Alive, Alonso sniffed for the sea.

Part IV

32

'Like all the rest of them,' she said, 'who cannot cope
with life, he took a turn with death, and when he thought
    his charm had won the day for him,
he set off climbing towards the light. But
    when he stopped, as we all knew that

33

he would, and looked back over his shoulder, he found
that I was not there; but then of course I never
    had been. It is not in my nature
to be a follower. Ah, but my nails
    were soon there when my Bacchantes

34

had run him down to earth. His thin ribs we stripped out,
clawed clean and scattered among the rocks. His singing
    head we sent down Hebrus. We quelled
the rebellion of the trees, and all
    the Lesbian coves incarnadined.

35
At Tintagel I lay listening to the waves
slapping against the red-stone walls of the castle,
    and my thoughts went out like black sails
billowing towards him over the sea.
    One morning especially I recalled

36
redolent of roses in a high-walled garden;
me in a pearl-white gown of soft silk from Toulouse
    and he embroidered as the May.
It was an ordinary garden
    with the usual blemishes:

37
thorns on the roses, a thistle or a nettle
here and there; but we two might well have walked our long
    love's day together there, had he
had eyes to see things as they really were
    and not forever tried to read

38
portents and omens in particularities,
so pestering me with obtuse parallels that,
    wearied, I brought him to the brink
of these Lethean waters, and kissed him
    hard through the silence of their fall.'

NEW MAPS FOR OLD

While once they were allowed
Some flighty bits on the side,

Maps now look to be meaning
At its most monogamous:

No cherubs; no Here Be Lions;
No galleons tilting in the bay.

Holding an increase in fact
To equal an increase in truth,

They ignore the traveller's need
To tell the lie of the land.

Their houses had been shaped out of the rock itself
on the north face of the bluffs
and in the deep shade of the overhang,
so that abseiling down from the *mesa*
proved to be as hazardous
as climbing up from the canyon bottom.

But once there,
brushing away the dry centuries of blown sand
was like cleaning a kitchen:
wooden dishes on the tables,
pestles, spoons and storage jars;
and a candlestick carved from a single
stem of juniper, with traces of scented beeswax
still hard-set in the bowl.

Their shallow refuse pits
gave evidence of a balanced diet.
And pollen analysis suggested
some previously unknown varieties
of celery and melon. The corn was mostly
yellow dent, with a little red-ear.

Yet nowhere in the vicinity was there a tilth
fit to scratch, let alone farm,
and none of the wherewithal to trade or barter.
What also went unnoticed at first
was the total lack of weapons, totems and toys.

It was only when Bradshaw,
pressing on into the living space,
found porcelain and bone china there
that they paused awhile in their work.

And then the animal paintings on the wall:
antelope, chamois and caribou;
the attention to detail casting doubt
on any suggestion of sympathetic magic;
those white violets clustered in the foreground,
and the frangipani and hibiscus.

The growing sense of intrusion
both men had remarked upon
was to be explained in the third chamber:
the body of a young woman –
not mummified or embalmed
but simply dried
owing to the high level of aridity.

Her long hair hung down over a shawl of feathers,
and though her skin had yellowed,
even the eyes were still in place,
'only,' as Northrop put it,
'the glint of life missing.'

She had on leather, square-toed sandals
and a loose-fitting garment
woven to a texture
of five hundred threads to the inch.

She was sitting on a stool
with her back against the wall.
She had been opening oysters.
And her left hand clasped that knife
which was to become the symbol
of their Travelling Exhibition:
the owl motif inlaid with silver,
the blade of obsidian.

KNOWING YOUR PLACE

Not far along the road that crosses
Kirkby Moor, there's a stand of sycamore,
A dozen or so, their tops rounded
And buffed by the wind. Then comes the long, slow
Slope of Benson's Hill on up to Horrace.

Away to the left, neglect has bewitched
A hawthorn hedge into a camel-train
Of trees climbing against the sky-line.
Horrace is a child's drawing of a house.
A right turn there takes you down to Lowick.

It's a walk I feel I have perfected.
I know the gate where the piebald ponies
Come dribbling down to have their noses rubbed;
Where brambles, as they die, take on the red
Of Indian leather, and where the Coniston Hills

Begin to unfold. One more right there
Brings you in no time to a tarn: Nut Hollow, or
Knotallow? No one seems sure. But a place
Is its own mind, and to know it truly
Is like knowing a poem: it isn't always

What the words mean that matters, but what is heard
In the silences – in the tension that exists
Between the pulls of memory and feeling.
From now on it is the sound of running water
That will be with me all the way down

To Newbiggin; to a farmhouse sheltered
By a tight fold in the hill, and built
Out of the hill. Making no claims to a view,
It is what is meant by belonging:
A collaboration and an atonement.

It was the Age of Reason.
And when spring broke in Selborne
And Timothy the tortoise did come forth

And march about, they had a feel
For his pulse, but could not find it;
Bawled at him through a speaking-trumpet
But he appeared not to regard it;

So they dunked him in a tub of water
To see if he could swim, and watched him
Go sinking down to scrabble on the bottom,
Quite out of his element, and seemingly

Much dismayed. But what puzzled them most
In Selborne was that Providence
Should have squandered longevity
On a reptile who relished it so little

As to spend two-thirds of its existence
In a joyless stupor, all but the thread
Of solstitial awareness suspended.

But there are lessons to be learned everywhere,
And as Timothy awoke with the first flight
Of the swallows, might not they too
Have their hybernacula?

And had not Dr Johnson himself seen them
Conglobulate, before throwing themselves
Under water, wherein they would winter
On the bed of the river?

Sometimes Timothy escaped them,
Toddling his carapace out through the wicket:
Pursuits of an amorous nature transporting him
Beyond the bounds of his usual gravity.

SKULLS

Down where the swash and backwash of the tide
Had retched up wet entanglements
Of bladder wrack and kelp, the usual
Goitred orange and a single shoe,
We found the dead gannet.

Its intricate, slim wings intact as when
We saw them fold like paper darts
And plunge into the seas round Boreray;
And still with that slight blush of yellow
To the head, like a girl's chin

When you hold a buttercup beneath it.
And I wanted that skull – the great beak
Longer than my longest finger – to put
Beside the hooked and sun-bleached hawk's
On my windowsill.

But lifting it I found the tongue gone
And a thick gruel of maggots
Already on the boil in its gullet,
And I couldn't touch it. We walked off
Talking of flowers instead:

Of the misty and paler-than-harebell blue
Of the sea-holly, Crippen's henbane,
And the trumpets of convolvulus
Like the horns of ancient gramophones
Shaped out of porcelain.

But looking back I saw how the wind lifted
One wing and let it flap and fall
Like Ahab's arm when the white whale sounded,
Breached and rolled. And I thought of others
That I had missed out on:

Those oiled razorbills at St Bees,
The rat-gnawed heron on the banks
Of the Nene, and I knew that the only way
To win skulls such as those would have been
To take a knife to them,

Slicing into feather and skin, probing
For the vertebrae, to sever
Cartilage and ligament and cut through
To the bone. It's either that or waiting
For the sea's gift, or the sun's.

FOR I WILL CONSIDER MY DOG TOBY

Yes, we were sold a pup in Peterborough
and we called you Toby.

You came in a box: a real old
orange box with a lid on,
and little fluffy tufts of hair
sticking out through the slats in the side.
By rights you should have been adorable –
all puppies are. But no, not you.
You hadn't, as the man put it
when he looked inside,
'travelled very well'. In fact,
you'd puked your price down
by almost half. I suppose we should
have been grateful.

Chewer of chairs, and puddler of carpets,
if your puppihood was predictable,
your teens were traumatic.
Well for me they were at least.
That day I saw you come trotting up the path
with a whole fresh doughnut in your teeth,
I knew then that we were in for trouble.
But couldn't you have just stayed a thief?
Specialised even in it a bit? Did you
have to try to kill van Ashfelt's chickens,
and chase his cows around the field
until you'd damn near buttered all their milk?
And sex. Now I grant you, Toby, that's not
an unreasonable need, but did you
have to keep on raping little Pooch?
I can't tell what you saw in her,
but this I do know – Mrs Vieth herself

is not a pretty lady, and her purple
apoplexy was something I found hard to take.
And what about pinning the postman to the hedge?
And the man who came to read the meter,
just how long had you held him prisoner
in the shed?

You had your good days of course –
like when we threw a stick into the river
and you ignored it, and came back
with a water-lily in your mouth
and dropped it at your mistress' feet.
There never was such canine gallantry,
and carried off with such panache.
You could do no wrong – not after that.
Compared with you, Sir Walter Raleigh
was a lout. But you were soon back
to your old ways again, and we'd clout you,
and try to shut you in the cellar.
One day I rang the Dogs' Home and booked you in.
I'd had enough.

       But we always forgave you
That hangdog look that you perfected,
and the big brown doleful eyes. No one could resist.
Yes, beast, I could and would forgive you anything,
except, that is, getting so sick; so sick
that yesterday I had to take you to the vet
and come home again with a full heart
and such an empty lead.

THE DAYS OF CREATION

'Hwæt sceal ic singan?'
Cwæð he: 'Sing me frumsceaft.'

I

IN THE BEGINNING

Hearth and sweat
The new art had as
Hearts and wheat.

A new start he had,
Star had new heat

Then Hades at war,
He at dawn's heart
Was at hand there

And saw that here
Death has a new art;

And what tears he
Shed: a heart-want.

And the water has…

And the heart was…

And the earth was
Without form and void
And the darkness was

And he cwæð

Let there be light.

II

No, I'm not at all sure about yesterday.
Today's alright. I mean,
I know where I am today.
I could tell when it began for one thing.
But I'm not sure whether yesterday
ever did begin, or whether I began;
or whether I've always been around;
or what *always* means for that matter,
or *matter* ...

I could tell when yesterday ended.
That was night.
I'm not sure I liked the night.
It was so dark – not at all
like before there wasn't any light.
But that's one of those things I'm already
finding it hard to remember.

Something moved upon my face.
And then there was light. I liked the light.
And I was really happy when it came back again.
That was when today began.
But even today hasn't been altogether good.
I've felt – how can I put it? – *divided*.

It looks as though there's another night coming.

Sometimes I think I know
how the hermit crab is going to feel.

III

And God said:

let there be a process
to be known as photosynthesis,
whereby the pigment chlorophyll,
by means of the radiant energy of the sun
will combine water with carbon dioxide
to produce sugar in the form of glucose,
at the same time giving off oxygen

and the Green Man said:

when I open
my mouth
I utter leaves

IV

It was Thursday morning already,
and so much still to be done, but
with muesli, toast and tea for breakfast now
He sat awhile and dreamed: of two small boys

playing in a rock pool, teasing the shrimps
and little scuttling things so contentedly
that until they heard it roar they never guessed
a lion, led by a lady all in white

was walking towards them over the hill.
'Let me weigh both your laughters,' she said,
'to tell which is the happier.'
But the scales twisted from her hands

into a scorpion, that bent its tail
as an archer would his bow. Sensing
a tragedy, He shifted in His sleep,
and dreamt up a goat with hoofs like hammers

to stamp on that scorpion; and then of Himself
as the children's father, coming from the house
with a bucket full of water to sluice
the mess away. The water went trickling

over the cobbles and down into the stream,
touching the tail of a trout that jumped,
and startled a ram into leaving its flock,
which caused a bull to abandon its herd

grazing on a cliff overlooking a beach
where two small boys … Enough! It's time for work.
But God, not wanting to forget His dream,
scribbled it across the sky in stars.

V

A BENEDICITE

'Through the mechanistic operation
of inanimate forces and by the power
of natural selection'
we have:

the cuttlefish, which expands
and contracts bags of yellow, brown,
orange and red pigments embedded in its skin
so as to change colour and blend
in with its background;

and the eye of the common newt,
whose lens, when removed surgically,
will grow again
from the edge of the iris;

and the bombardier beetle,
which defends itself
by squirting out a jet
of noxious benzoquinones
at a temperature of
100 degrees centigrade;

and the male emperor moth
which can detect a female
emperor moth by her smell
at a distance of
eleven kilometres, up wind;

and that series of small peristaltic pumps
arranged along the oesophagus of the giraffe
which enable it to lift water
up to the required height of three metres
when it is standing, head-down
and legs-straddled, drinking;

and the in-built thermometer
of the Snowy Tree Cricket:
add 40 to the number of chirps
it emits in any period of fifteen seconds
and you have the exact air temperature
in degrees Fahrenheit.

For these, and so much more,
O, 'Mechanistic Operation',
we give thee thanks.

VI

THE LAST PAT FROM THE POTTER

'I have said enough,' said God.

'I want there to be other tongues
to tell me about the taste
of the honey and the salt;

about the feel of linen to their fingerpads;

about the forest's variations
on my theme of green;

and about onions and soot;

I want to know what someone thinks
about the way the thunder sounds,
the way the waves speak.'

It was the last pat from the potter.

'I have left a little
of myself in this,' said God.
'When it comes to its senses,
I want to hear from it.'

SOME INITIAL STEPS

Supposing he was right, Pascal:
    and that all our miseries
    do stem from an inability
    to sit quietly in our own rooms?
       Perhaps I won't go.

And yet Kierkegaard held that
    if 'one just keeps on walking
    everything will be all right,'
    and we do *take steps*
       to solve a problem.

Now 'walking is the natural recreation
    for a man who desires not absolutely
    to suppress his intellect,
    but to turn it out to play for a season.'
       And that from Virginia Woolf's father.

The scandal of pedestrianism,
    according to De Quincey,
    is 'more happily situated than that
    of scrofula or leprosy; it is not
    in any case written on your face.'
       More writing.

In ancient Egypt
    the hieroglyph for the soul
    was a pair of legs – walking.

A country diversion, insisted Millamant,
    'I nauseate it'
       but you can walk anywhere
       if you've got the time.

God walked in the garden
        and Wordsworth along a gravel path
        so that 'the continuity of his verse
        met with no collateral interruption.'
            Except from Hazlitt.

Only those thoughts we have
        while walking:
        laufenden thoughts, said Nietzsche,
        are of any value.
            It must be time to go now.

RONCEVAUX/RONCESVALLES

Tear-stained with rain, these beech trees
give a wistful note to the wind,
like that of a distant horn.

Voyez les ports et les détroits passages

This is the frontier of truth
and myth. And truth will have it Crescent
and Cross were not at question here.

Haut sont les puys and les vaux ténébreux

No bold Crusader, Charlemagne;
he'd gone freebooting for the Saracens,
till double-crossed and piqued, he turned

En douce France s'en repairera le Roi

and trekked back home again – stopping just once,
so his moody troops could sack
and ransack Basque Pamplona.

Et Sarrasins qui tant sont assemblés

And that's what did it. They were Basques
waiting on the heights of Roncesvalles
while the oriflamme whirled by;

Quatre cents muls chargés de l'or d'Arabe

Basques who dropped down on the baggage-train,
the ox-carts, pack-mules, carpenters
and cooks, and massacred the lot.

'Dieu!' dit le Roi, 'si peineuse est ma vie!'

Such ignominy the chroniclers pooh-poohed.
Losses were few: Anselm, Count Palatine,
and Roland, Warden of the Breton March.

Ci faut la Geste que Turoldus décline.

PAMPLONA

July was once simply
the feria of San Fermin,
himself martyred on the horns of a bull.
These days it's the bust of Hemingway whose scowl
gores the aficionados at the bull-ring.

And down by the river,
as the sun rises, it kindles
a restless chafing of hooves in the dark
fetor of the corral; then you hear the brisk
sound of the cornet and drum as the bands come

threading into the square.
The streets seethe: a jostle of white
scarfed in scarlet. Barriers are in place;
and anticipation pulls on the long gap
like a toothache. At the first stroke of eight

the rocket. And the bulls
are out there already running
up Santo Domingo, then swinging left,
horns down, hooking, bunching into the narrows
of the Estafeta. Ahead of them

the headstrong, the macho
and the maverick, charge hell-bent
for the encierro, where in the blanched
heat of the arena, a matador will
lift his bull through bravura de pechos,

then spin it and turn it
in tightening chicuelinas,
the low, slow sweep of the veronica;
the faena and kill: thick embroideries
of blood trailing behind it in the sand.

*   *   *   *

While on the other side
of the city a plaque: 'Aquí
cayo herido, San Ignacio
Loyola' marks the spot where he fell, wounded:
soldier then – neither Jesuit nor saint,

but sanctified, it seems,
by a ball that splintered his leg
when the armies of France besieged Navarre.
The leg set by surgeons, broken and re-set,
his mind fought at the barriers of pain,

where, moved by stillness, he heard
in that immaculate silence,
the rallying call to a new standard.
Ad Majorem Dei Gloriam, he wrote.
A beggar had his cape; the church his sword.

PUENTE LA REINA

'Y desde aquí todos los caminos
a Santiago se hacen uno.'

And three statues greet the four roads.

First, the pilgrim, on his plinth, barefoot,
though that broad-brimmed hat of his,
the stolid staff and capacious cloak
declare him a man of substance.

St James looks ruffled and windblown;
is dusty, anxious-eyed.

While in La Iglesia del Crucifijo
the body of Christ slumps forward
on a Y-shaped
arm-breaking cross.

There is still a long way to go.

Three statues and four roads. And six arches
to carry this queen of bridges over the river.

Below, a moorhen slowly
prods its way against the stream.
The water is flood-yellow.

A sudden freshet of rain lifts that
savour of new rope from the cobbles.

Storm-clouds have bruised the hills.

On the parapet someone has left
a rose-hip, two blackberries,
an almond and some purple heads of clover.

Once over the bridge
the road veers sharply to the right,
and I know that from now on
I will be 'stepping westward'.

EASTER SUNDAY AT SANTO DOMINGO
DE LA CALZADA

No thanks to Saint Dominic of the Causeway.
A hard coming I've had of it, foot-sore, soaked
And exhausted, like hundreds of thousands before me,
But the legendary cockerel cooped up
In the cathedral crows me its greeting.

The legend goes like this: a young pilgrim
Was hanged for a crime that he didn't commit,
But his parents (the Saints preserve us)
Found he was still alive on the gibbet
And went running to tell the magistrate.

He, deep into his supper, scoffed at them.
'Alive?' he said. 'Alive as this roast chicken!'
And the bird, as was only to be expected,
Got up on its feet and promptly crowed.
Rooster and saint are since inseparable.

A lady tells me that this one crowed
Fourteen times during last week's sermon.
Once was enough on another occasion.
I'll take the fish tonight. Someone put to death
Last Friday is, I believe, alive again.

CHECKS AND BALANCES

What I don't know is why I didn't give up

When the rain fell outside Puente la Reina
And the old road ran into a quag
Of new roadworks, so that for over a mile
I had to stop every half minute or so to scrape
Coagulations of sludge from my boots

And when I got lost again and again
Between those yellow crumbling villages
Beyond the Rio Oja, and yet another
Pack of half-starved dogs, lips curled
And snarling, came leaping and gnashing at me

And when my own folly and bravado tempted me
To try and cram two full days' walk into one
And the last six miles into Burgos
Were a dual carriageway, and the buffetings
From the lorries battered all the breath out of me

But I do know, if I had, I'd have missed

A long, quiet walk over the meseta;
Frost crisp underfoot; the sky an unbroken blue;
Larksong; watching my shadow slowly shorten
And edge towards the north; feeling my shoulders
Warm to the sun, and hearing that first cicada.

FROMISTA

A dry walk along the side of a slow canal.
Another town. Another plaza mayor.
Another statue. Another saint.

But who's this one who looks to be blessing the world
While riding towards us on a surfboard?
San Telmo, his plinth says. San Telmo?

I've never… No, wait, we've jumbled up the Spanish.
This must be Saint Elmo. He of the fire
That glowed from the harpoons Ahab held.

But what can the patron saint of sailors
Be doing here in the wide wheat fields of Spain?
My guidebook tells me it's because he was martyred

By having his intestines winched out of him
On a windlass. Dear God, is the imagination
Of man never so fertile as when

We are inflicting pain on one another?

LEÓN

This, in my eyes, is the great cathedral.
Proof that actuality need not always
Be the impoverishment of what is possible.

In its Gothic fragility it holds back
From Baroque's magniloquent contempt for tact.

I sit and watch the shadows of the nesting storks.
Like holy ghosts, they rise and fall
Behind the stained-glass windows of the choir.

With three rose-windows, and over two
Hundred storied and decorated panes
It sometimes seems that there's more glass than stone.

But late of an afternoon, when the sun
Rings in through these golds, these greens, these reds,
And through this lapis blue, it can feel

As though it is neither glass nor stone,
But the light itself that sustains it all.

OUTSIDE VILLAFRANCA DEL BIERZO

For a moment I felt like Robert Frost:
There being two roads to choose from,
But the one less-travelled-by
Looked private too.

      I stood there, uncertain
And conspicuous, and an old man in crumpled
Beret and carpet slippers came tottering
Towards me. 'Hola,' I said. 'Can I take
Either of these paths?'

      'How can I answer
Such a question,' he barked, 'when I don't know
Where you are going to, or why?'

      God damn it.
Another time warp. I'd gone and got myself
My own leech-gather now. Lost for words,
I took the Frost road in a rush and headed
For a fold in the hills.

      There was hibiscus
Growing there and I saw my first
Hoopoe, but could not shake
That old man from my mind. At every bend
In the turnings of my thoughts he came back at me,
Like some ancient Taoist, his beard
White now, his hands tucked inside his sleeves.
Sometimes he was positively Jungian.

One thing I could be sure of: he'd be waiting
To have another go at me on the way down.
But I'd get him this time. I'd be

On the other road for a start. And I was.
And so was he, jabbing the gravel with his stick.

It was a challenge, I knew that. 'Well?' he said.
'Absolutely marvellous,' I replied,
Trying to hint that he'd missed out on something,
Stuck down here beside his house all day.
Then, and this was my big ploy, adding
Enigmatically, 'And I have been
Where I have been.' I'd practiced it. *He ido*
Adónde he ido. But he, with the gesture
Of one throwing a peseta to a beggar,
Said, 'Hombre, isn't that always the way?'

DUST

The rain has stopped now that I am in Galicia,
And the mud-ruts in the lanes are baked and dried.
Even so, I keep on seeing that same
Bootprint. All the way from Pamplona
It's been with me; sometimes so fresh I've felt
Certain to meet up with whoever made it
Over the next hill, but never have.

What's one though, when this road is deep
With the footprints of the dead? Everywhere
You look, someone who went before has left
His mark: be it that little ivory crucifix
In León, whose Christ seemed quite contented
On his cross, smiling and wearing a skull-cap;
Or the great Gothic cathedrals themselves.

Each swirl of dust that clouds up round my feet
Assumes a separate and momentary shape.
Watching them, one might well be led to think
That it was the spirit of the dust
That travelled, enhanced and quickened
Into something complex and more strange,
But falling, it settles and is dust again.

Exhausted or exultant, there is no avoiding
The ghosts of those who plodded along this road:
per lo cammino alto e silvestro.
Like them I cursed the incessant rain
As I climbed up through the Pyrenees,
And knew the purgatory of seeming not to move
As I trekked across the high plains of Castile.

There are destinations which demand
That we ourselves have been the journey,
And it is some way yet to Santiago.
Maybe I've brought too much: guide books and maps
Can blur the edge of our uncertainties.
Travelling on with a trust in what was there,
They walked their faith. I walk their elegy.

AT THE TOMB OF SAINT JAMES

Now whether his body is in the tomb or not
Is only a question of matter,
So scarcely matters, and it is hard to say

Whether the absence of his presence
Or the presence of his absence
Is now the more palpable;

Or whether it is the gathering
And gathered resonance of us all
That echoes and creates.

AT SAMOS: A QUESTION

'And what wood are you made of, my son?'
It wasn't a question. I could tell that.
He was a Benedictine, and much taken
By my walking-stick: the slim, ebony

Look to it, its sleek, swept-back
Dog's-head handle: sad-eyed and with a touch
Of the lugubrious about the jaw-line.
I had bought it in the Grand Bazaar

In Istanbul, and had myself been taken,
And taken in by it too. It wasn't
Until I got home that I realised
That it was in fact just lacquered bamboo.

But I'd walked over three hundred miles with it
In three weeks, and the monk was impressed.
No, it wasn't a question. I knew that.
All the same I wish he hadn't asked it.

ENDINGS

Now that I am here, I ask myself why.
      I had not expected
any kind of epiphany, knowing that when I came
      to Mateo's
Portico de Gloria, that the smiles on the lips
      of the saints

would stay stony, the hurdy-gurdy dumb.
      I would, even so,
have welcomed a sign, if not of praise, at least
      of recognition
that something had happened. Was it different then
      for those who came

in the their scallop hats and sandal shoon? Did they
      run all the way
from the top of Mount Joy, believing that below them
      lay the Heavenly City?
Was it for them not just a road but an allegory?
      It is tempting to think so.

In the hope that myth may sometimes define
      our intuitions
of reality, we are always happy to give house-room
      to any suggestion
that there is a point to what we are doing: a charm
      against the haphazard;

so the insinuations of travel become ever more Dantean:
      the cold and the wet
of the Pyrenees, that long trudge across the meseta,
      the deep green lanes of Galicia,
and finally a cathedral whose granite does seem
      to shimmer with gold-dust.

Still, this sense of let-down. Such reach of purpose
          hones awareness,
until you know that any final step would be
          a rehearsal
for death, but that is a step as resistant
          to metaphor as it is

to reason. We set out and we return. And we set out
          for something which never
has been reached, because to do so is to go beyond it,
          and we return
to something within us which has never come into being
          nor ever passed away.

All other offers of certainty are as evasive
          as those small
flurries and scatters of birds that keep drifting on
          just ahead of you
down the whole length of a hedgerow when you are
          out there walking.

from THE BENDING OF THE BOW
A retelling of the closing books of The Odyssey
{A FIGHT}

But the day's dramas weren't done with yet. As luck
    would have it, into the hall at that moment
came a real beggar, the most notorious
    beggar in all of Ithaca; huge chap
he was, but with a great beer-belly on him.
    The suitors all called him *Iris*, because
he used to run (if that was the word) messages
    for them.
        But he wasn't a man who would
tolerate rivals.
        'Come on, old 'un, out of it.
On your way now. I know it would amuse
    my friends here to see me throw you out on your neck,
    but there's no need for it to come to that.
I'm not the sort to look for trouble. So just get!'

    Odysseus glared at him.
                        'I don't think
I've said or done anything to annoy you, friend.
    Have I? There's room enough for two of us
to make a living here. We're both in the same plight
    after all, and I wouldn't begrudge you
anything you could get. But don't push me too far,
    or I might just bloody your nose for you.'

'Eh? You what? I'll knock your teeth all over the floor.
    You want a fight? You want to take me on?
All right, let's show these gentlemen what you can do.'

    Antinous heard them and laughed out loud.
'Well, this beats everything! If those two old beggars
    aren't going to have a scrap! This we must see!'

And they all jumped up and crowded round them, cheering.
      'Listen, my friends.' It was Antinous
again. 'I've got an idea. Whoever wins
      this noble contest, the *best* man, as it were,
will henceforth dine with us, and he will be our own
      personal beggar, to the exclusion
of all others!'

      The rest roared their approval.

      Odysseus – *crafty* – that was the word
that people used when they talked about him – then said,
      'He's a younger man; it's not a fair match.
It's only hunger drives me to this, you know that.
      But I want you to promise me something:
no one's to take his side – I want no sneaky blows
      coming in my direction.'
                              They all gave
their word, and Telemachus added,
      'Have no fear,
      anyone who joins in will have the rest of us
to contend with.'

                        Odysseus began
      tucking his rags into his belt, and it was
then the suitors saw the size of his legs, his chest,
      the width of his shoulders, and the muscles
on his arms. (Athene was near by, adding a touch
      extra here and there.) They nudged each other.
'Look at the body on that man. This could be the end
      of Iris. Serves him right. He started it.'

Iris saw him too, but Antinous stepped in.
      'Listen to me, you fat fool,' he sneered.
'You're probably wishing you'd never been born,
      aren't you? A little nervous are we? Eh?
Well I tell you this straight: if he wins, you're going
      on the next black ship to King Echetos.
And you know what he'll, don't you? Skin you alive
      he will; cut off your nose and your ears;
and rip your bollocks off and feed them to his dogs!'

      Poor Iris was trembling so much now
they almost had to hold him up. Odysseus
      was trying to make up his mind whether
to kill him outright or just damage him a bit.
      In the end he decided it wouldn't
be wise to call too much attention to himself,
      and so, as Iris moved in, he chopped him
with a quick backhand under the ear. He felt
      the bones go, and down went Iris; blood came
bubbling out of his mouth, and he lay where he fell,
      whimpering, his legs twitching in the dust.

The gallant suitors could hardly stand for laughing.

      Odysseus dragged his man off, dumped him
up against the wall in the doorway and then said,
      'You stay there, and don't try it on again;
or you might not be quite so lucky next time.'

      The suitors were still laughing. They gathered
round him, slapping him on the back, and one pronounced,
      'Stranger, for this I pray to all the gods
in heaven that they grant you your heart's desire.'
And Odysseus liked the sound of that.

{A RECONCILIATION}

    Penelope wondered as she went towards
the stairs, what she would do when she saw this husband:
    whether she would stand aloof a little,
or whether she would run and kiss him straight away.
    What she did in fact was to go and sit
in a chair by the fire on the opposite side
    of the room. He himself was sitting
by one of the great pillars, his eyes on the ground,
    waiting to see what she would say when she
saw him. But she said nothing. Sometimes she looked up
    and glanced towards him, but it was as though
she didn't know him.

            Telemachus could take it
no longer.
      'Mother, what are you doing?
Why don't you at least speak to him? It's twenty years
    he's been away. How can you be so hard?'

'I'm not being hard, child. But what can I say?
    I'm lost for words. But if he truly is
Odysseus, we will know each other, and we
    won't have need of words; there are signs, tokens,
that are known only to us.'

          Odysseus smiled.
    'Don't rush her. Let your mother take her time.
It's probably that I'm so dirty, and dressed in
    these smelly old rags that she won't talk to me.'

Meanwhile a bath had been made ready for him.
     Servants washed him, bathed him and anointed
him with oil. They brought new clothes for him to wear,
     and Pallas Athene even added
a touch herself, making him just that little bit
     more handsome, maybe an inch or so taller,
and curling his hair as tightly as the petals
     on a hyacinth, so that when he stepped
from his bath you would have said Odysseus
     was a god.

     He went back and sat down
on the same chair as before; and waited; then spoke.
     'You are a strange woman,' he said. 'I don't
believe anyone could be as hard-hearted as you.
     Who else could just sit there and say nothing
when her husband had been away for twenty years?
     Eurycleia, you can make up a bed
for me out here. I'll sleep in the hall alone.'

     Then Penelope answered him. 'It's you
who are the stranger. I'm not being hard or proud,
     but I remember so clearly
what you – he rather – looked like the day he sailed
     from Ithaca. But never mind.
                              Eurycleia,
get some men to carry the bed out of my room
     for him and put some covers on it here.'
Crafty – that was the word people might have used
     about Penelope then.
                              Odysseus
exploded in a rage.

                    'Woman,' he shouted, *'what*

did you say? How could that bed come to be moved?
It would take something more than mortal to shift that.
    I made it and I know. In the courtyard
when we came here, there was an olive tree growing.
    Its trunk was massive. I built our bedroom
around it. I built the walls and roofed it over.
    Then I trimmed the branches off and smoothed
it with an adze. That tree I made the post of *our* bed.
    I made the bed too; inlaid it with gold,
and silver and ivory – lashed it together
    with thongs of oxhide dyed in purple.
That should be token enough for you, I think.
    But what I want to know from you, woman,
is if that bed is still there in its place, or if
    some new man has cut it at the root?'

Penelope ran to her husband and kissed him.

    'Don't be angry with me, Odysseus,'
she said, 'that I didn't welcome you as soon as I
    saw you. It was the gods kept us apart
and I was always fearful they might send someone
    to deceive me.'

            When Poseidon, the god
of the sea, goes after a well-built ship with wind
    and wave; smashes it, and sinks it, and drowns
almost the entire crew, you can imagine
    how happy the survivors are as they
struggle through the surf, caked with brine, and finally
    scramble up the beach –
             well Penelope
was every bit as happy as that. Her white arms
    were around his neck and she would not let go.

They sat and talked.

                    Meanwhile Eurynome,
working by firelight, had put out soft blankets
     for them and laid bright coverlets upon the bed.

And then when all was ready, she led them to their room,
     to joy in the old ways of their love.

Tap-tapping with his pencil
like blind Pew,
it crossed his mind how often
words had led him into areas
as menacing and unmapped
as any of the polar wastes
the likes of Frobisher
and Franklin sailed to.

So fragile their barques,
ambition chafed against survival.
Could iron and creaking oak
hold out against water,
wind and ice; compass
and chart contend
with snow and fog; could
ingenuity outwit this wild?

Certain shallow bays and attendant
headlands having been found
and named, they headed for home.
Crouching in their cabins, their journals
cradled against the pitch
and yaw, they searched for words
to relate the groaning
of the floes, the winds' howling.

TIDELINES

Holy Island

> *– the swan's down feather,*
> *That stands upon the swell at full tide,*
> *And neither way inclines.*
>
> Antony and Cleopatra III. ii. 48-50

1

Beginnings can be difficult.
Even so, had I begun with that line
in the days of Eadfrith, Cuthbert, Bede,
I wouldn't have got this far yet.
I'd still be pricking vellum for my initial
B; letting the plump O's of it
billow out over the page, and its long stem
fall further and further down the edge
like a mare's tail, like kelp, like candlewax,
like some thick round midwinter icicle.

2

You've seen the way a sheepdog
comes across a field with that low,
rippling, crouching sort of run they have,
threatening a nip to every jostling
heel of the flock they're driving?
Well, this morning's neap tide was like that,
menacing its way over the mudflats
and setting up such a panic
among sandpiper, plover and knot
that they were all flickering in and out
of the lacings and leavings of it
as if nothing quite like this
had ever happened to them before.

3

This, naturally, would have been nothing new
to any apprentice of Eadfrith. His rule
ran as inexorably as the tides:
the tablets of wax their craft was learned on
needed to be pristine smooth again
each morning; interlace went the way
of worm-casts; vowels and consonants
like footprints of the birds. Sound practice,
he insisted, likewise a lesson in humility.
Nothing lasts in this world. What was it he'd seen once
doodled down a margin somewhere: 'Whirl is King!'?

4

plant becomes fish
fish beast and beast bird
in this gorgeous zoomorphic
interlace of spiral and curve
branch feather and fin
interwoven in a celebration
of creation where we can see
plant become fish
fish beast and beast bird
in this gorgeous zoomorphic
interlace of spiral and curve
branch feather and fin
interwoven in a celebration
of creation where we can see
plant become fish

5

For all that it's axe-shaped,
flourishing its blade in the face of the North Sea,
Lindisfarne succumbs, must give ground
twice a day as the waters come in
over the causeway; and cut it off.
And not only in space – time too.
This afternoon there is no past here – no *harrying
of the heathen* in these invasions of the tide;
it's just water, just the rattle and drag
of shingle, something that's happening now.

6

Far out, a wave is little more than a slight
darkening of the water, a suspicion
of shadow; a deepening of the blue
that swells slowly; growing into a grey
wall of water that rises and rises until it's
so high it over-reaches itself, topples
and falls, breaking into fragments of foam.

7

So much cobble and shingle. Sandstone
I can recognise – granite and slate. And over there's
what's surely a piece of smoothed-off
house brick; but these others, the dull, round
grey ones – they must have names too.
And down among the grit and gravel
(never mind the shells) there's such
carmine and cadmium, such amber and
(who knows?) pearl, and not one bit of it
altogether accident – each with a history
of the collisions and contingencies
that have broken, shaped and burnished them,
as they judder backwards and forwards
between the grandeur and futility of it all.

8

They could be eider: Cuddy's ducks,
but with this low-sun, high-wind
faceting of the waves it's hard to tell;
in fact it's hard to settle on anything
with these gusts of gulls being
blown about across a mackerel sky.
Whirl, it seems, is truly king today.

Looking over towards the low
outline of Hob Thrush, Cuthbert's Island,
the stories surface; as otters did
coming out of the sea to warm
and dry his feet after he'd stood
all night praying waist-deep
in the waves off Coldingham;

and those ravens, thatch-thieves,
bringing him lumps of lard in recompense
to waterproof his boots. Stories
that keep their hold on us
but drove him, with their risk
of fame, to his beehive hermitage
on Inner Farne, and the sky and the sea,

and the sea and the dry land. Balanced
on this margin and threshold of the world,
he could hold out against the tidal
pull and push of self – his life pared and honed so
it flourished among the thrift and samphire,
Peter's herb, along the shoreline; moments
stilled to rock-pools where the small

quick shadows of translucent things
scurried under stones – a stasis so total
and complete the sea itself could not
compete with it, though I saw it try once
in Rusland Pool: the tide
wrestling against the strength of the river
and the river fighting to hold it back,

and for perhaps half a minute it seemed
they called a truce – such a calm
settled, it was as if the present
had overlapped both past and future:
the swan's down feather. But the river,
catching the sea off guard began nudging it slowly
back again to where it rightfully belongs.

Barefoot we crossed the sands to Lindisfarne.

THE ALHAMBRA, GRANADA

Once at least it seemed to them,
the navigators and explorers,
(it was in the South Arabian seas
where the scent of aloes reached them
on an offshore breeze)
that they had come very close to finding Eden,

but when finally they gave up in despair,
agreeing, what ought
to have been obvious from the start,
that the Flood had doubtless swept
all trace of it away,
then one by one their patrons,

men of imagination and of wealth,
decided it was time to build,
each for himself, a paradise on earth,
so the ships were all laid up,
maps stowed away and gardeners sought
to re-create that home

their hearts all hungered for,
where they could enjoy the shade
of their own vines, breathe in the fragrance
of jasmine and hear the splash
of fountains in the evening;
the ancient feeling of estrangement overcome

at last, and put to rest
with never a wilting leaf
or any of entropy's transactions
permitted to intrude
on what might otherwise have proved
to be such a good place to die in.

THE VILLA D'ESTE

Shears and secateurs are in command here:
any extravagant inclination towards growth
gets clipped right back into line. Order prevails

in a controlled opulence, which His Eminence
perhaps saw as being yet one more triumph
over chaos, where whatsoever was barbaric,

or hostile, or simply less than perfect
had been wisely, firmly and finally walled out.
From the top of the grand staircase it is still

possible to catch a glimpse of the Campagna,
but on the way down our eyes are held
by alleys of gravel, scroll-works of box,

hard-edged laurel, ilex and yew; and stone;
stone everywhere; stone walls, stone benches,
terraces with balustrades and statues,

fountains, where water is flung time and again
high into the air and sculpted into fantasies.
Less the work of gardeners than of

architects, outdoors here seems to be only
one more aspect of what went on indoors,
and pre-eminently an assertion of will,

a symbol of power. Twice though,
having lost our way on a lower level,
we came face to face with the same defunct

fountain, left to dribble over what might once
have been Bacchus, but now had become a green
grotesque: slime running down its belly;

a rank stench of mildew; lichen and moss
sprouting out of his nose, his ears, his mouth. We both
knew him in an instant; knew that the Green Man
had somehow climbed back in over the wall.

IN THE CHELSEA PHYSIC GARDEN

It's early days yet in the Cool House:
there are new ferns with their heads curled
as tight as crosiers, while others,
taking after the horsetails are not only
up, but already so rampant
we look like having the whole
of the primeval swamp here soon in bonsai.

Being a gathering together, it would seem,
of the scattered shards of that First Eden,
this rhetorical landscape does not preserve
only what's pretty – hence the sundew
that upset Ruskin so, and the deadly dewlap
of the Pitcher Plant, some kinds of which, it's said,
trap and digest small reptiles, even rats –

or only what's exotic: it is oddly
reassuring to come across rhubarb here,
but to find a dandelion is somehow shocking;
usually they grow at the whim of the wind,
in the lawn, or in cracks between paving stones;
this one though has a nameplate all of its own
so demands that it be looked at, not just seen,

that we try to recognise the truth
of it, not the truth about it; responding
to its sheer incandescent explosion
of yellow, yet, at the same time, aware
that each individual petal
is straight-edged as a chisel. Being
uncertain is what mostly makes us

wonder. Seldom permitted
the chance simply to look, we know
what's coming; and in this case it's
the geometrical miracle of that seed head,
the blow-away clock. There is no
such thing as immaculate perception
where everything's myth, everywhere caprice.

TOUCH WOOD

Touch Wood, we say,
hoping it'll bring us luck,
and as luck would have it, today
I have only to put down my book
and step outdoors to be in a wood;
sycamore and ash, maple and oak,
and no two trees ever the same.

Trees don't even burn the same.
Some are generous with their heat,
but give it out slowly,
while others crackle and spit sparks
so in next to no time you're outside
filling the log-basket up again.

Their bark can be so different too:
from the scaly furrows of the larch
to the smooth, dark grey of the beech –
beech being a name that shares
the same root (notice the metaphor)
as the Old English word for *book.*
No, we're not out of the woods yet.

In Ireland I was told that the first man
came from an alder tree, the first
woman from the rowan, or mountain ash;
and once there was a law that anyone
who did violence to a tree
should be decapitated on its stump.

Trees outlive us, and we envy them
their permanence. There never was
a tree that looked unsightly, and nothing
else on earth can be said
to still look beautiful when it's dead.

It's when trees do die though
that they can sometimes
be a tad erratic: playing host
to so many different kinds of fungus –
some like frost and some like toffee-apples.
One I saw looked as crusty
as a new brown loaf
and beside it was a tiny blob
the colour of ripe cheddar.

And they are the trees that fall.
Those that are felled, dried
and seasoned get cherished
lovingly. Sawn and planed
to a finish that's silken to the thumb,
they are the ones that furnish our lives,
the ones that will outlast us, and the ones
which may, mercifully, one day become
a coffin for relatives to hide
our own unlovely putrefaction in.
Touch wood.

WILLIAM AND ADAM

No one could claim they have had it easy,
William and Adam, the two
chubby-legged stone cherubs
now gracing our narrow, damp back garden.

They could never have imagined themselves
ending up like this: on their uppers
one might say, if they had any.

Two hundred years ago
would have seen them glancing shyly
from some herbaceous border,
wide-crinolined Cassandras
and Carolines floating by.

What a come-down.

Even so, they've known worse.
Both at some time
had their heads knocked off;
an anti-cherubic faction
of the *sans-culottes* maybe.

But then things did get better.
Someone, seeing their plight, took pity
and mended them, so cack-handedly though
(which is why we got them cheap)
that each now looks to be wearing
a concrete woolly muffler round his neck.

They need them too in this weather.
After breakfast I noticed
the trumpet of a daffodil
resting against William's ear
like an old-time telephone;
and Adam, that winsome smile of his,
turned towards him, suggesting:
'I think it might be someone for me.'

A MANDATE

To all intents he was a tender gardener.
He turned the soil, secured the trellis
to the wall, and twined the tendrils

of the seedling sweet-peas through it
as they grew; yet he himself was up
and gone before the hawthorn was in bloom,

and heading westwards (the candles
of the sweet-peas flickered out and died)
and then still west and west again

until it came to him some flowers he passed
he'd never seen before, like this small yellow one;
with something of the poppy to it

but only half the size, yet not a celandine.
And the birds, even the little brown birds,
he couldn't name; it was a locale

rinsed of the accretions of habit,
of innuendo, even of surmise; somewhere
waiting to be seen for what it is;

as if Adam had been allowed back into Eden
with a pocket full of labels, and a mandate
that he re-enchant the world.

RELIQUARIES

Not a complete shell, just a broken
water-polished piece of one, but the more
precious for that, being all I could find,

so I brought it back to put alongside
the blue-jay's feather and the acorns
I picked up while out walking yesterday.

Why we keep on doing this it's hard to tell.
These acorns I like, I know, because of
the raggedy-knitted berets that they wear,

but in themselves, the stones, the feathers
and the sprigs of lichen are nothing special.
Maybe we re-invent them: allow

them meanings; or slowly they tell us
what their meanings are; metaphors or icons
possibly; somewhere a god might be

persuaded, or engage to come. They come
and go of course: lichens crumble and stones
tend sometimes to look much like stones.

Some may become things we can't be parted from,
but they too get put out with the rubbish
by strangers or by daughters when we die.

THE ROAD TO THE GUNPOWDER HOUSE

This is where it begins:
this footbridge over the throat of the estuary,
where the Crake and the Leven roil
under the inrush of the tide,
and pale swirls of ochre silt come rising up
to explode and blossom in the flow.

The hawthorn isn't yet in flower,
but there are catkins out on the hazels,
and the other side of the river,
in Roudsea Wood,
where the path bends to the right,
you get an earlier glimpse of the shoreline
since that broad stand of timber
has been felled and cleared.

It's always quiet here.
Thick wads of felt were tied to the hooves
of the horses hauling the wagons
up and down this track:
one struck spark would have been enough.

But that's all dead and done with now:
gunpowder, horses, mines.
The four-square, stout-walled powderhouse
has been reformed into a rustic somewhere
for the Cavendish to host
a summer evening's barbecue.

Through the window you see logs
piled tidily by the fireplace, wicker chairs

and bottles choked with gutterings of wax.
The door's been shut tight all winter.
Some eavesdropping spider
has spun a web across the keyhole.
It too is alive
to the possibilities of explosion.

OVID IN EXILE

Late afternoon
until early evening, as on every other
late afternoon and early evening,
he stood and watched the waves,
one after another, shuffling unstoppably ashore.

Mere cats' paws they were mostly,
but nine such, he'd been warned,
unleashed a tenth with tow enough
to maul and claw you under.

Well, and why not?
One's exit should have some panache;
and better that than the peremptory
botch-up they'd likely give him in Tomis.

Exile. As if getting old
weren't exile enough in itself;
though he of all people surely
should have seen that metamorphosis coming.

Memories ambushed his mind:
how her wind-teased tresses turned to green leaves
as Apollo's hands reached out
to take her; strands become twigs
and Daphne safely and forever laurel.

Now there were no trees, and no girls either.
What he had instead was what he thought
he'd always wanted, and that was time.

Like a thing taken for granted,
the earth turned through a blizzard of stars.

Time – that plumps the grape
but dulls the plough – he'd wasted
looking for ships; waiting for letters;
he might as well have tried to till the sand,
littered as it was with shells, the way words
littered his lines; pretty to look at,
but the life gone out of them.

A curlew called from the dunes.

As he'd said to Severus once:
writing a poem with no one to read it
was like dancing in the dark.

A finger of cloud smudged out the moon.

But what could he do?
He clapped his hands and he shuffled
his feet and he danced – danced
like a man garnering the sun.

Why of course. There wasn't the slightest
hesitation. A mother and child
might very well (yes, Mrs Ramsay even,
sitting at her window)
be reduced, she rattled on,
to a triangular purple shadow,
just there, just there, you see,
without demeaning them.

Each mass, each highlight, depth and texture
required the balance of its counterpoint.
She began to sense herself believing this.
And so reality
was what you made of it. James
was slowly prising loose a flake of paint
with his fingernail
while his mother read

aloud to him in the fisherman's
gruff voice, and Lily, out there in the garden,
stood quiet now, beside her easel,
wishing for one of those
moments which by running
so very counter to reality
had somehow almost
reconciled her to it.

And having dibbed and dabbled long enough
among the umbers and the blues, she raised
her brush, held it poised, and like an angel
on a pinhead tried
to balance, even to dance
a few light steps upon it, but she failed.
'Women can't paint.' Why then
persist, teetering on

jostled so by such inconsequence?
A skimpy little thing, she'd heard one say,
who'd never marry and would never sit
like Mrs Ramsay
in a window seat,
her son upon her lap and read to him.
no one would ensconce her
in a purple shadow.

And so she wiped her brushes on a rag
and tidied everything away. And as she did
she sang a little to herself, quite wordlessly,
but they heard her, and heard
how through the rhythms
of what might otherwise have proved a dirge,
she intertwined some grace notes
of incorrigible hope.

ATTICS

One of my ambitions is to have lived
as a child in a house with an attic,
the sort you get to up a narrow
wooden staircase – bare boards, no carpet –
the sort of staircase with a sharp bend in it
just five or six steps below a shabby door
that swings shut behind you on its sneck

attics are where things end up that no one
wants, but no one thinks to throw away:
boxes of photographs, long-tasselled lampshades,
a tennis racquet with a fish-tail handle

attics are where bachelor uncles
who went aboard, never to return,
left behind their *personal possessions*

attics are where stories start, where letters
are found, and lonely, sensitive children
make discoveries about themselves

I will, it seems, have missed out on this,
driving to the tip with bits and pieces
I could have safely stowed upstairs,
to be stumbled on sometime by someone
who would laugh and call out, 'You really have
to take a look at this,' or quietly
to themselves, say, 'Oh, now I understand.'

WOMAN STANDING IN A DOORWAY

Dreams had been playing
at ducks and drakes with her
half the night, skittering her
in and out of shallow sleep,

until at last she'd given in
and come downstairs,
leant back against the doorway,
propped one foot up behind her,

settled her shoulders and folded
her arms. Not a pose Vermeer
would have favoured, more
a Murillo; not that it mattered,

not when the entire garden
looked to have re-composed itself
in the time it had taken her
to unlatch the door.

Moon-bleached, it was so still,
so quiet and so new. What had been
weeds were wild flowers,
flowering wildly among the scented

pomp of bloom and trimmed box.
An unlooked-for grace it was,
she felt, to be there at all,
and by herself, able to just stand

and look at this thing
or at that: the sun rising;
a billhook left out overnight
in the wet grass; the blood

and rust of dahlias by the path.
A moment to treasure. Nothing
unusual, nothing… hadn't she
heard somewhere the first

dahlias had come from Mexico?
That they'd been Aztec flowers?
Those painted priests, frightful
in their feathers, had her held down

and were reaching for the billhook
when the peacock morning
screamed out before her and she
was on her feet, brushing something

off her skirt, as sunlight
ruffled her hair and from the kitchen
came the smell of toast
and the sound of coffee being made.

Sitting in the little outdoor café
she mostly favoured, Valeska's
on the corner of the Träumenstrasse,
its six blue tables each with a
tall glass of dwarf delphinium,

she found she couldn't settle;
if she wasn't fingering her scarf
she was twizzling her spoon about
inside her cup, or cutting her pastry
into tiny cubes. Too many of her mornings

were tending to begin this way of late;
she might have been an actress
standing in the wings, waiting, anxious,
listening for a cue that never came.
But a triumphant carillon

then rang out, bang on cue, and she glanced up
just in time to see a shock-head David
jump from a Gothic door and punctually
slay Goliath, as the clock in the tower
of the Rathaus chimed the hour.

And she thought how, if she could
only freeze and fix one moment,
mount it as one would a butterfly
so as to study it, to take a long
close look at it, complete

in its totality, that would make
all the difference, would make sense
of the most ordinary of things:
the patterns the starlings made when they
exploded like scatter-shot from the roof-tops

would then become to her as treasures
salvaged from a shipwrecked-dream.
But they were already settling back
on every gable end; clouds had occupied
the hilltops and an avalanche of shadows

fallen and engulfed the market place,
snuffing out the blue delphiniums. Yes,
things change. That they do was something
you could always count on, and there was,
she supposed, comfort of a sort in that.

THE METAPHYSICS OF TULIPS

The latter falls in love, and
reads Spinoza …
                    T. S. Eliot

It was of course a joy for her to hear
the trumpets of the daffodils blare out
so brazenly around the house each spring.
It never had occurred to her to touch them though,
whereas, with tulips, their smooth round firmnesses
she couldn't help but stroke, softly and gently
with the backs of her fingers, from tip to stem,
the rich deep colours waxed so gorgeously.

Dull old Dr Johnson had said something,
hadn't he once, about not counting
the streaks inside a tulip? It wasn't
to be done, but she thought she would
to see if like the speckled patterns
in the gorge of foxgloves there were never
any two the same, like it was claimed
of snowflakes, which was a hard one to believe.

No, it wasn't getting any easier
these days, seeing things for what they were,
but then that Jew who fled from Portugal –
the one who polished lenses, wrote a treatise
on the rainbow and reasoned that *a free man thinks*
of nothing less than death – he never understood
when he got to Amsterdam, why it was
the onions tasted so insipid there.

Now it may well be, in the long history
of our crowded universe, that her joy
or lack of joy, were two infinitesimally
small events, but this was her table in her
kitchen, and this was the chipped blue vase
her mother gave her; the tulips had all come
out of her own garden, and she did
so love the moist and silky feel to them.

THE BLESSED FOOL

Of the generation of the third son
he is – one of those whom we find it all too easy
to disparage, while we still
have the one with the brains,
and his brother with the muscles
to see us through when trouble comes.

But it isn't only in fables
that these two have unloosed
such a frenzy through their failures
that the heresy of the fool
was all we had to turn to: his modest
and yet inviolable quiet of the spirit.

It may then be only wise, with the old
ceremonies drifting into apathy,
to reinvent the great Feast Day
of All Fools: to set it aside
as a time for the piling of irrational gifts
on the doorsteps of strangers;

as a day for the veneration of doodlers
and dreamers; and when evening comes,
one might perhaps invite the Fool Himself
to dance for us, with steps
and gestures of an awkward
tenderness, his understanding of sorrow.

It's on the right, no more than a yard or so
before High Sunbrick Farm as you come up
over Birkrigg from Ulverston. In truth though
when you get there, there isn't anything to see:
just another scrubby little paddock
behind a drystone wall; a bed of nettles,
a few thistles. But the plaque by the gate
says this was once a Quaker Burial Ground
and Margaret Fox (née Fell) was buried there.

But that's all. There never was a headstone
to show exactly where. For the Friends, the body
being at best but a dark lantern
to the inner light of the soul, to draw
attention to it would have seemed like vanity,
and that, they knew, was only one step short
off wantonness. And now I think of it,
I told a wanton lie myself when I said
there wasn't anything to see up here.

What's sure to stop you stone dead in your tracks
is the Parkers' whim of keeping peacocks
on their farm. Flaunting those plumed tiaras
on their heads, they must be the swaggering
antithesis of everything that Sunbrick
and the Man in Leather Breeches entertained
when they spread their tails, flutter
the lustrous iridescence of those eyes,
and dance their stately, slow pavan.

It's doubtful whether Margaret ever danced,
but it's to be hoped she saw the way the light
catches Bardsea steeplehouse as the dark
rain clouds come bruising their underbellies
over Ingleborough; and the changing
patterns of their shadows on the wet sands;
and those autumn evenings when the sunset
the far side of the bay looks like slices
of peaches. It is to be hoped she did.

THE FOUR HORSES

I

A white horse fidgets on a hill,
tilts one hind hoof forward,
then settles. The rider fusses gently
with its mane; shifts a little in his saddle.
Both are beginning to lose interest
in the fires and carnage in the valley.

II

If there was ever a time when the sun
was the flank of a blood-red horse
galloping down over the rim of the world,
it was seeing these men grinning and shoving in
to be photographed around the corpse
of a man they'd all but flayed.

III

'One measure of wheat for a penny!'
Hawkers and tinkers from way back
they'd been, the whole family, he said.
Times might, it's true, look bad, but thanks be
they still had Shadow – bonny nag – and the cart.
And it was a job needed doing: 'Bring out your dead!'

IV

Their fires spent, these sit on in darkness,
a defeated people. Obstinately alive,
they cough and shiver. Outside, drifts of snow
crouch, then scurry about their houses.
Soon the last of the riders will arrive,
reining in his pale horse at their doors.

Though nothing but a shadow of itself,
there never was the shadow of a doubt
it was the fossil of a crocodile
they had unearthed at Kettleness. At first sight,
with its bones and scales so perfectly intact,
it looked to her as if it had been stitched
inside the stone, an ancient petroglyph
somehow become embroidery.

Then Sunday came, and the truths of scripture
took a hammer to geology: *though they be hid
in the bottom of the sea, thence will I command
my serpent and he will bite them*; preached
with scarcely a thought for the women
whose menfolk might even then have been tumbling
through a tangled welter of rigging and spars,
past blunt, grey fish, to the sea's floor.

Sensing that she was beginning to skitter
and slide a little down Caedmon's Trod
in her hurry to get away from there,
she steadied herself and took a hold of the wall,
let herself gradually become aware
of the wind on her face, the clamour
of the gulls, and the little Whitby cobbles
going about their business in the harbour.

Twenty million years ago, they said, it had lived here,
and she could picture them – a great plume of years
stretching out behind her like a comet's tail.
But with so few, she had begun to fear, still left
ahead of her, what use were they, any more
than these new continents that men had blundered on,
when day by day and year by year she'd sat
sewing at this same window and in this same chair?

WHAT DO WE HAVE BUT HOPE? was the motto,
set within a frieze of gaudy birds and flowers,
she'd worked at as a child. First one stitch
and then another she unpicked until
every one of them was gone. She did toy
with the notion of using her one last strand
of dark green silk to form, in tiny
running stitches, the knuckled outline

of the crocodile, but it was getting dark.
October had already come and gone,
tipping the black spot into the yellowing
outstretched palms of the sycamores that grew
behind the house. Rain rapped at the glass,
and there was a sigh from the wind as though
trying to tell her things which she was
by no means certain she had any wish to hear.

FOURTEEN STEPS ALONG THE EDGE

ONE

Almost the last, their Christmas card, all guilt
with Angels, brought tidings of his coming death;
but eastwards towards Norwich I went, bearing gifts
of gloves and paperbacks and soap; wishing
I could share her confident: *all manner
of things shall be well.* Poor sparrow...

Edwin himself, that bitter Yule-tide in the mead-hall,
couldn't be sure whether it had been a thane's
gift with words, or if he'd really seen it
fluttering past him in the firelight.
Either way, the blizzard bared its teeth.
'No one gets out of life alive.'

TWO

Just as there may be a river we've never reached
but know for sure to be there from the twists
and turns in a distant line of willows,
so the insinuations of a reality we cannot face
the mind explores and re-creates
in images: Acheron, Lethe, Styx.

And isn't it then through the lyricisms
of loss that we begin to sense
the tenderness of impermanence?
You remember how we saw the New Year in
at Baycliff, by the water's edge, while the slow
constellations wheeled on by overhead?

THREE

What with the soil frozen so hard – stones
impacted like molars – you could hone
a scythe on my front garden this morning;
yet for all that, six or seven green
spathes of snowdrop have somehow slid themselves
through with not a mark on them.

Delicate deceivers. We look out for them
time after time, as though we were a part
of that world of renewal and return;
in hope whereof last year she intertwined
his winter-fingers with their pale heads
to carry with him through into the dark.

FOUR

In the brown depths – lustrous as seaweed –
of my daughter's eyes, I remember
my mother's; and in the opportunities
of the one: San Francisco, Istanbul,
realise now the frustrations – sheets to wash
and shopping to carry – of the other.

Midway between them, I would, as things go,
expect when I die to be fairly content
with the way things went; but conscious still
of the faint shadow of an only son –
so only as to have miscarried
before we had chance to set eyes on one another.

FIVE

There was this man coming home from work.
Simon his name was. Not looking for trouble.
If he'd thought on, he'd have gone the other way
and not got mixed up in any of it,
but the centurion, he said, 'Hey, you, buggerlugs,
give him a hand with that; he can't cope with it.'

It was some terrorist too. Well, anyway,
that was why when he did get home his clothes
were all mussed up and there was this great bruise
on his shoulder. Said he didn't want to talk
about it; except he did say you never can tell
just when something's going to come and clobber you.

SIX

The pollen checks looked hopeful: a type of
desert tamarix, native to Palestine;
the fear was carbon-14 tests
coming up with a date of fourteen hundred
and proving it fake. How then to believe
what our eyes had seen: the body of a man

scourged and crowned with thorns and crucified?
That such a death was not unique was not the point.
The miracle lay surely in what else we saw:
the folded hands, the dignity, the peace
and the awesome serenity of that face:
that this too was a man – *in imaginem dei.*

SEVEN

Not death, but the dying. It was raining
and the streets were thick with mud when they dragged
Campion on a hurdle from the Tower to Tyburn,
where they hanged him, cut him down, chopped off
his privy parts, disembowelled and beheaded him.
then hacked up what was left into quarters.

For Margot, death came in the private ward
of a Barrow hospital. First one leg,
then the other they amputated.
Mercifully unconsciousness had intervened.
She had no teeth in and was incontinent.
If only I had made it to her funeral.

EIGHT

A child's face lies among the shoes
and second-hand dresses on a stall.
This was Sarajevo's 'Massacre
of the Market Place' – alliteration
soothing it towards fiction and oblivion.
But the past persists. It is where

precedents take place; though God alone
knows what new hell this could presage?
'Weep for your children,' he told the daughters
of Jerusalem, 'for if they do these things
in a green tree, what shall be done in the dry?'
His assumption being there would still be trees.

NINE

Eager for coherence, I am always
gladdened by the mind's ability
to make beauty – if not sense –
out of the teeming particularities
that strafe us like meteorites;
but events of late have proved a problem.

It's not just recession, terrorist attacks
and toxic spillage; there were those mudslides
after the earthquake; fraud, scandal and theft;
bushfires, shipwrecks; and deaths of course
by various and gruesome kinds of violence.
What Lent can follow such a Mardi Gras?

TEN

Memory teaches us to remember
(There was snow on the beach, and ice. The sea
had gone, leaving this token of itself behind)
but no one as yet has found the way to forget.
The future you might expect to arrive
like an incoming tide; but this tide's been here before.

This is no sacrament to wash us clean.
The old rope and guilt, the humiliation
and plastic we flung into it yesterday
comes back again. This is our inheritance.
The past will drench us in our own detritus.
Waves strip the bone white and leave it on the shore.

ELEVEN

If I'd dared to prise open his hands
I'd have seen the pale half-moons his fingernails
had made where he'd been clenching them so hard.
That would have told me something. I could have gone
with him to the water's edge and walked
by his side (these fourteen steps at least)

watching the smoke-grey ripples of sea-snipe
turning to silver; hearing the curlews cry
among the dunes and in the shallows; and this
before he left for where the white gannets wheel
and soar, stretching their slim wings out wide
against the sky as they turn and dive   dive   dive

TWELVE

When the bleep stops and the green line lies down flat
on the electroencephalograph
that's death. It used to be held to be breath:
breathing out the air we'd breathed in at our birth.
'This feather stirs; she lives!' But Lear was wrong.
Cordelia's breath would mist no stone again.

Heart-breaking? And a heart-break that must feel
as physical as the fingers on the wrist
where no pulse beats. But it's the head
against the heart that tells us – the phenomena
of the mind – and ultimately in the mind
of whichever of us is left behind to grieve.

THIRTEEN

Yes. Yes, you can. You can imagine it.
It's like when you take an uncooked chicken
out of the fridge – well perhaps not quite so cold –
that's the way a corpse feels – and it's not nice.
You know straight away something's missing,
something we conspire to call life.

And yet – as with the pietà – that kiss,
sweet to the lips if bitter to the taste,
love has never flinched from. Our feelings
for the dead don't fade because they're dead:
they fade because we ourselves are losing
in the struggle against impermanence.

FOURTEEN

Mindful of the ships in bottles he had made –
cold rain splattering into the grave –
I smashed one to pieces on a tombstone,
set fire to the bowsprit and the rigging,
and with himself lying in state on the quarterdeck
sent it sailing proudly away down the runnels …

Just once to have countered dust and ashes
with: And thus they buried Hector, tamer of horses;
or: Winter has passed, *et flores*
apparuerunt in terra nostra – by some such
attestation of worth at least
to make peace with the certitude of loss.